Watch Your Tongue

What Our Everyday Sayings and Idioms ~~Literally~~ Figuratively Mean

Mark Abley

Illustrations by Belle Wuthrich

Published by Simon & Schuster

New York   London   Toronto   Sydney   New Delhi

SIMON &
SCHUSTER
CANADA

Simon & Schuster Canada
A Division of Simon & Schuster, Inc.
166 King Street East, Suite 300
Toronto, Ontario M5A 1J3

This Simon & Schuster Canada edition October 2018

SIMON & SCHUSTER CANADA and colophon
are trademarks of Simon & Schuster, Inc.

For information about special discounts for bulk purchases,
please contact Simon & Schuster Special Sales at
1-800-268-3216 or CustomerService@simonandschuster.ca

Manufactured in the United States of America

Illustrations by Belle Wuthrich (www.bellewuthrich.com)

1   3   5   7   9   10   8   6   4   2

Library and Archives Canada Cataloguing in Publication

Abley, Mark, 1955–, author
Watch your tongue : what our everyday sayings
and idioms figuratively mean / Mark Abley.
Issued in print and electronic formats.
ISBN 978-1-5011-7228-1 (softcover).—ISBN 978-1-5011-7229-8 (ebook)
1. English language—Idioms. 2. English language—Terms and
phrases. 3. English language—History. 4. English language—
Social aspects. 5. Clichés. 6. Figures of speech. I. Title.

PE1460.A25 2018   428   C2018-902314-7
                                      C2018-902315-5

ISBN 978-1-5011-7228-1
ISBN 978-1-5011-7229-8 (ebook)

For all the teachers
who give their students the chance
to find joy in words

Contents

Key to Sidebars

Combing the Giraffe

Foreign idioms

Donkey's Hind Leg

Outdated idioms

Household Names

Idioms from names

It Is Written

Biblical idioms

Merchant of Words

Idioms from Shakespeare

Spoonfuls of Sugar

Language trivia

 Tomatoes on Your Eyes

Nonsense idioms

Raining Glass

It was a blue winter day in downtown Montreal, and I was standing among thousands of other shivering people on the city's main shopping street. We had gathered in solidarity with the Women's March on Washington, the day after the inauguration of Donald Trump as US president. A local gaggle of the activist group the Raging Grannies sang a homemade ditty to the tune of "Oh! Susanna"—"Women's power, we're here to make a stir / Don't mess around with women's rights, we roar as well as purr." Cat motifs were in evidence throughout the rally, notably in the form of knitted, pink "pussy hats"—a response to the incoming president's vulgar boasting about his sexual conquests.

What struck me, as I looked around, was the language on the hundreds of cardboard placards. Some were direct and blatant anti-Trump slogans. But many of the signs, like the grannies' song, used more subtle, idiomatic language to make their point. "Pussy hat" was itself an idiom, and one big sign hoisted by a woman standing a few yards away from me said, "Pussy grabs back." Placards reading "Love is power," "The future has no gender" and "Walls won't divide us" seemed like optimistic attempts to spread new proverbs. "Girls just want to have fundamental rights" was a clear spin-off from the old Cyndi Lauper hit "Girls Just Want to Have Fun." "Post-Truth = Lies" made a terse comment on a recently coined expression, "post-truth."

My favorite placard, being waved to and fro in the cold air as the Raging Grannies warbled on, read: "I won't stop till it rains glass." It was a brilliant play on words. But unless you grasped the meaning of the expression "glass ceiling"—the invisible, powerful barrier that Hillary Clinton had hoped to shatter—the sign would have made no sense.

The language play so noticeable on these signs was evidence of hope, I thought. Even at a time of immense concern about the future, hundreds of people at the rally had gone to the trouble of making placards that displayed a frisky, defiant creativity. Gatherings in other cities brought forth equally inventive signs: "Free Melania," "He shall overcomb," "Keep your tiny hands off my human rights," and so on. The people who invented these expressions and held these signs were refusing to let anxiety or depression override their urge to find words adequate for the challenge.

That's a very human impulse, one with a long and glorious

history. Soldiers in the trenches during the First World War scribbled away in damp notebooks. Prisoners in Nazi concentration camps and the Stalinist gulag wrote on whatever materials they could find: scraps of paper, candy wrappers, toilet paper, even stone walls. Human beings are creatures of language. We speak, therefore we are.

And when we speak or write, we often resort to idioms. We use words not just in a factual way—"Don't let the dog off the leash"—but also in an idiomatic way: "Don't be a dog in the manger." Idioms are small artifacts of imagination. They encapsulate and sum up aspects of our experience. Whatever genre they fall into—miniature poems, sermons, jokes or warnings—they can keep time in abeyance. Clothes and furnishings, even those from recent years, are regularly consigned to the thrift store or the garbage, but idioms from the distant past still trickle through our lips and ears. Many English expressions that are familiar today ("dog in the manger" among them) were well known in the Middle Ages or the Renaissance.

Language is always evolving, but some of these idioms show an impressive capacity to resist change. Ever since William Shakespeare was a child, long before Samuel de Champlain or the Pilgrim Fathers set off across the Atlantic, a selfish or spiteful person has been said to take a dog-in-the-manger view. Never a cat in the manger. Never a dog in the stable. Never two dogs in the manger.

Not all idioms survive, of course. Technological change has rendered many of them obsolete. It's only members of a rapidly aging generation who are likely to recall what a "Kodak moment" is, or was. Likewise, the expression "Hold your horses!" made sense in previous centuries, when horses were abundant in cities and a necessity of rural life. A person who offered this advice to the driver of a wagon or cart—or to anyone else—was saying, "Be patient! Slow down!" But to shout "Hold your horses!" in the twenty-first century would be to sound irredeemably old-fashioned.

Linguistic obsolescence can also affect the online realm, where expressions that were up to the minute a few years ago can now seem hopelessly dated. When was the last time you heard anyone announce what they discovered while "web surfing"? Several organizations select a new "word of the year," a choice that often turns out to be not a single word but an idiom. Since 2007 the words of the year as picked by *Macquarie Dictionary* have included such duds as "phantom vibration syndrome," "googleganger" and "pod slurping." Tech-based vocabulary can have an amazingly short life span.

Donkey's Hind Leg

In October 1993, an article in the *New York Times* stated: "One of the technologies Vice President Al Gore is pushing is the information superhighway, which will link everyone at home or office to everything else—movies and television shows, shopping services, electronic mail and huge collections of data." The American Dialect Society chose "information superhighway" as its word of the year for 1993. The idiom seemed destined for a glamorous future.

Not so. "Information superhighway" shot to prominence but remained in wide use for less than a decade. Then it disappeared. The number of its appearances in a major Canadian newspaper, the *Vancouver Sun*, traces its fate. "Information superhighway" entered the *Sun* in 1993, when four articles contained the phrase. In 1994, the expression appeared in sixty articles; the following year, thirty-one. The total kept on falling until 2002, when it wasn't mentioned at all. The road had run out.

Nobody knows which of the idioms introduced or favored by millennials will be alive in the language two or three generations from now. Predictions are rash. But I'll "go out on a limb," to adopt an old expression, and say that Inc.com's 2015 list of "15 Words and Phrases Millennials Use but No One Else Understands" featured several expressions that won't stick around for long. One of the top items was "hundo p" (one hundred percent). It would be a surprise if that phrase outlasted a couple of the more useful expressions on the list: "Sorry not sorry" (a partial or insincere apology) and "The struggle is real" (serious annoyance).

Idioms are, by their nature, acts of fusion. They bring two or more disparate elements together into a single whole. They embrace metaphors, similes, proverbs, analogies—a whole range of imaginative thought. "Language is not something which could be built up one word at a time," the philosopher Charles Taylor argued in his book *The Language Animal*. "Each word supposes a whole of language to give it its full force as . . . an expressive gesture." If that's the case for individual words, it's even more so for idioms. Often, on a word-by-word basis, they make no literal sense.

I'm using the word *literal* in a traditional manner. To many people, even today, a statement is "literally" true only if it's free of all metaphor and exaggeration. But just as the verb "dust" can mean either to clean the dust away or to sprinkle something with dust, "literally" now has a pair of opposite meanings. In 2011 the *Oxford English Dictionary* added a new sense to its definition of the word: "Used to indicate that some (frequently conventional) metaphorical or hyperbolical expression is to be taken in the strongest admissible sense." When reporters noticed the change and asked for comment, one of the dictionary's senior editors, Fiona McPherson, dryly remarked, "It seems to have literally slipped in under the radar." Still, I prefer to maintain the old distinction. Just as I've never heard a dog barking in a manger, I have never "literally died laughing."

The implications of a phrase like "glass ceiling" have nothing to do with the architectural meaning. Similarly, the walking dead—as far as I'm aware—do not inhabit shopping malls. But when a long commercial building sits nearly empty, most of its stores and restaurants having closed down, the place becomes a "zombie mall." This is a young idiom, one that has not yet reached many dictionaries. Nonetheless, the *New York Times* used the expression in a memorable headline in April 2017: "From 'Zombie Malls' to Bonobos: What America's Retail Transformation Looks Like." The risk of such headlines is that for some readers, the "wow factor" will be overtaken by the "huh? factor."

Every word or phrase depends on context. "Bonobos," in the *Times* headline, refers not to small, endangered chimpanzees but to an "e-commerce-driven" chain of men's clothing stores. "Own the school year like a hero" may or may not be a smart expression for Walmart to display in its back-to-school advertising, but when a Walmart store in Indiana brandished the slogan in big capital letters above a gun cabinet, the context was wildly inappropriate. "Walls won't divide us" is a clear and powerful statement, but its implications are different in North America today than they were in West Berlin during the 1980s.

In short, idioms are more than the sum of their individual parts—they rely on "a whole of language" to convey their point. And although it may not be obvious at first, plenty of idioms have a moral or political edge. They're not as value-free as they may appear. "Three plus eight is eleven" is innocent, but it's not an idiom. "Am I my brother's keeper?" is an idiom, but it's not innocent. Neither are phrases like "illegal alien" and "death tax." In repeating any expression that touches on public issues and debates, we implicitly take some kind of stand.

Used with care and imagination, idioms can feed your head. "In China, the stool pigeon is the true hero of the revolution":

that's a line from a 2017 book review in the *Washington Post*. The reviewer, John Pomfret, was outlining the long history of surveillance practices by the Communist regime—not the most alluring topic, you might think. But his unexpected use of the American idiom "stool pigeon"—a term for a police informer— in the context of Maoist and post-Maoist China crystallized a significant idea in a few words.

Most idioms are specific to their own language. No matter how expressive an image they create, that image may dissolve on foreign lips and tongues—this is one of the main reasons why translation is such a difficult and necessary art. If you "show water to someone," what could you possibly mean? In English, the phrase is nonsensical. But in the Tamil language of southern India and Sri Lanka, it means to make an opponent dizzy, or to be that person's nemesis. Without having heard the expression before, we lack the means to see beyond the veil of words, so to speak, and grasp the idea the Tamil image conveys.

Combing the Giraffe

"I follow my friend to Gangnam" is an idiom familiar in both South and North Korea—Gangnam, the site of a smash-hit video by the South Korean musician Psy, is a district of Seoul. In South Korea, the expression is said to mean "I'm following my friend's desires, not my own." In the North, the idiom had a related though slightly different meaning. But in 2013, the regime suddenly banned its use. The reason: North Koreans had begun to say "I follow my friend to Gangnam" when they really meant "I'm going to leave the country."

The ability of idioms to sum up an issue in a short, sharp way makes them appealing to editors who are paid to write headlines. This is a tricky craft, because stories are often complex and space is always limited. On a random Monday in the summer of 2017, I checked the *Wall Street Journal* to see if its headline writers had used any idioms. Indeed they had. A story in the fitness section suggesting that frequent visitors to gyms are now driving less had the headline: "Work the Abs or Fill the Tank?" In the business pages, an article on trends in beer consumption was introduced by "Brewers Can Get a Buzz from Low- and No-Alcohol Beer," and a report on stock-market lethargy appeared below "The Dow Moves at a Snail's Pace." An editorial about rogue traders for J.P. Morgan was titled "The Morgan Whale That Got Away." And on the *Journal*'s front page, a story about the problems facing Australian politicians with dual citizenship came with a catchy but misleading headline: "Australia Wants to Drain the Swamp—of Canadians."

Changes in policy are both signaled and symbolized by changes in language. In the first weeks of the Trump administration, staff in the US Department of Agriculture were told to avoid all mention of "climate change" and to use the expression "weather extremes" instead. Climate change is a stark reality—and a contested idiom. The staff were also instructed to abandon the expression "reduce greenhouse gases" in favor of phrases like "build soil organic matter" and "increase nutrient use efficiency." As the French philosopher Jean-Paul Sartre once observed, "Every word has repercussions. Every silence, too."

Idioms serve a variety of other purposes. For one thing, they add humor to language. There's nothing funny about saying "He's stupid," and on occasion, directness is what you may need. But often it's wiser—less offensive and more inventive—to say "He's sharp as a bowling ball." Or "He's a few sandwiches short of a picnic." Or "His cheese has slipped off his cracker." Or "He's as quick as a tortoise on Prozac." Or any one of the countless other idioms for stupidity.

Hour by hour, much of the language that comes our way is purely transactional—in their routine efficiency, the words have no discernible color or flavor. Perhaps it has to be that way. When you're staring at a business invoice, you don't expect to meet expressions like "sell like hotcakes" or "buy straw hats in winter." But invoices, memos, agendas, board minutes, job applications, order forms and the like are written with a single limited purpose in view. They have no other life. Any idioms that stray into them are as out of place as whales in a creek.

News stories, too, are supposed to state in direct, unbiased prose what a reader or viewer needs to know: "Just the facts, ma'am." (That's the tradition, anyway. In the current political realm, it risks becoming obsolete.) When a reporter is sent to the scene of a major fire, her job is to provide straightforward information about when the blaze began, how long it lasted, how much was destroyed, if there were casualties, and so on. She is not encouraged to write a story that begins: "Great balls of fire!" This may explain, I suppose, why most news articles are no sooner read than forgotten. It also helps explain why headlines that aim to entice people into reading an article rely sometimes on idioms.

Compared to reporters and executives, fiction writers have far greater latitude to use language in the most vivid, original manner they can—to make their words "leap off the page," so to speak. One of the most productive techniques for achieving this is the judicious use of idioms. I think of the Mississippi writer Eudora Welty. In a disturbing short story from 1963, "Where Is the Voice Coming From?," she enters the mind of a frustrated bigot who murders a black civil rights leader. The tale is markedly evocative because of the man's expressions: "fixed on me like a preacher's eyeballs when he's yelling 'Are you saved?' "; "trees hanging them pones of bloom like split watermelon"; "may try to railroad me into the electric chair"; "so hot to my feet I might've been walking the barrel of my gun." Desolate perceptions like these are at the story's heart. Welty's idioms awaken both our senses and our appalled imaginations.

As "Where Is the Voice Coming From?" demonstrates, the most powerful expressions are sometimes rooted in a single region. "Think global, act local" is a maxim that urges people to take action in their own communities for the sake of the greater good. For authors, it could be adapted to "Think global, write local." Despite the power of Hollywood, Wall Street and the internet to smooth out distinctions among the major dialects of English, differences persist. Indeed, the British and North American versions of an expression are often distinct. The Old World's "storm in a teacup" lasts no longer than the New World's "tempest in a teapot," and an English "spanner in the works" is just as annoying as an American "monkey wrench."

The English language continues to grow apace not just in the United States, Britain, Canada, and a few other wealthy countries, but also in parts of Asia and Africa. Works of imagination that are set in India or Nigeria, say, can be authentic only if their characters speak in voices that are true to their own place. These works may demand the use of local idioms. For example, Salman Rushdie's celebrated novel *Midnight's Children* is crammed full of passages like this one: "Amma, do not go to see other men, with Lucknow-work on their shirt; enough, my mother, of teacup-kissery! I am in long trousers now, and may speak to you as a man." It's not just particular images and expressions that evoke India ("Lucknow-work" is a style of embroidery popular in the state of Uttar Pradesh), it's also the rhythms of Rushdie's idiomatic language that distinguish *Midnight's Children* from North American and British novels.

Combing the Giraffe

"It's Greek to me" means "I just don't understand." For English speakers, at least. Speakers of Czech and other Slavic languages say "To me, this is a Spanish village," while speakers of Spanish say "This is in Chinese." What's foreign is a perennial source of suspicion. Some English speakers make the faux request "Pardon my French" before they unleash a swear word or an off-color joke, even though the offending expression has nothing to do with the language of France.

But no people get beaten up in the English language as often as the Dutch. You show "Dutch courage" only if you've been drinking; a "Dutch treat" is no treat at all; the "Dutch cure" is suicide. Admittedly, "double Dutch" refers to a harmless game with a skipping rope. But that expression can also mean gibberish. When a language is Greek to you, its speakers are talking double Dutch.

Figurative language has clout. But it needs to be handled with grace, and authors in any country are wise to abstain from the sloppy overuse of idioms. In a *Maclean's* article published in August 2017, the novelist Joseph Boyden mixed his metaphors at an alarming rate: "As an honorary witness, my personal mandate is to speak in my role as a writer and public voice about the dark clouds and frightening basements of our shared history and the abomination that was residential schools and the ongoing intergenerational tsunami of trauma." Public voices, dark clouds, frightening basements and intergenerational tsunamis probably don't belong in the same paragraph, let alone the same sentence. Idioms express a relationship, and they need to be in relationship with each other. Otherwise, a writer's work may come across as mere "smoke and mirrors."

Language is so essential to human experience, we should expect to find idioms that reflect its power. And sure enough, dozens of English expressions involve words and speech. Many of them illuminate the ways we look on language. These idioms "speak volumes" about how people communicate, or fail to do so. They are, if you like, the selfies English has taken of itself.

When two people have similar beliefs, or find themselves in agreement, they're said to "speak the same language." To convey the feeling more emphatically or enthusiastically, you might want to say: "You're speaking my language!" A third idiom that shows warm agreement is "Now you're talking." This phrase can also be used to express surprise. In John le Carré's 2010 novel *Our Kind of Traitor*, a British operative named Hector Meredith muses to himself, "Catch the minnows, but leave the sharks in the water. A chap's laundering a couple of million? He's a bloody crook. Call in the regulators, put him in irons. But a few *billion*? Now you're talking." The richly idiomatic nature of the language reflects Hector's inner agitation.

When a word or idea "rolls off the tongue," it's easy to say. A "silver-tongued" orator is someone blessed with "the gift of the gab." But idioms about tongues are not always so positive. A "tongue-lashing" is a verbal attack. If a scolding is profane or over-the-top, the person administering it might be told to "keep a civil tongue in his head." Or if you're keen to make a request but you're nervous about the potential consequences, it might be wise to "hold your tongue"—or "bite your tongue"—and stay quiet.

"Silence is golden," we're informed. It's rare to hear the original version of this saying: "Speech is silver, but silence is golden." Be that as it may, English has a variety of idioms to evoke silence and the occasional need for it. When you're "tight-lipped," you refuse to tell anyone what you know. "My lips are sealed": in that case, you won't betray any secrets. You're "as silent as the grave." Then again, if you remain speechless for too long, a questioner might ask disparagingly, "Cat got your tongue?"

Any doubts these idioms display about the value of silence are matched, or exceeded, by doubts about speaking too forcefully. It's never good to be "talking somebody's head off," for instance. In its scorn for excessive or careless speech, that expression is close in meaning to the even stronger idioms "run off at the mouth" and "shoot off at the mouth." Keep on like this, and I'll be forced to give you "a piece of my mind" or "a good talking-to"—a stern lecture, that is. A tireless talker makes it hard for anyone else to "get a word in edgeways." If you speak unusually fast, you "talk a mile a minute"—a remarkably quick pace, given that no human has ever run a mile in less than three minutes and forty-three seconds.

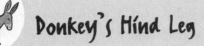

Donkey's Hind Leg

In *The Surprise*, a play by the English author G. K. Chesterton, a poet tells a princess, "There is always something that we have to say." The princess slyly retorts that the poet is never at a loss for words. To which the poet replies: "Oh, I know I talk the hind leg off a donkey—a very useless thing to do to a very useful thing like a donkey." It's a rueful admission that he talks too much and too long.

"Talking the hind leg off a donkey" was a commonplace idiom in the nineteenth and early twentieth centuries. Another expression, "donkey's years," meant an extremely long time. Neither idiom has logic on its side—but until farmers got rid of their donkeys, both idioms were widespread.

Untrustworthy people "talk out of both sides of the mouth" or "speak with a forked tongue." Why forked? It's sometimes claimed that indigenous Americans are the source of this expression. Addressing the Muscogee Creek nation in 1829, the newly elected US president Andrew Jackson said, "I love my white and red children, and always speak straight, and not with a forked tongue." A few years later, the Muscogee Creek were ethnically cleansed from their traditional lands in a forced march that became known as the Trail of Tears—so Jackson's tongue had indeed been forked. But in any case, the expression was not an American one. It has appeared in English literature going back to the seventeenth century, with reference to the devil.

Our vocabulary for taste is paltry compared to our vocabulary for deception. Either a food is sweet, or it's not. Either a food is salty, or it's not. But forked tongues and speaking out of both sides of the mouth are just two of the many idioms that involve false or misleading language. We "pay lip service to an ideal" if our actions don't match our fine words. We "lie by omission" when we choose to ignore an important part of the story. We use "weasel words" to avoid making a direct statement—weasels can supposedly suck out the contents of an egg while leaving the shell intact. "Barefaced lies" are the most blatant form, whereas "white lies" are the most benign, often uttered for reasons of diplomacy or kindness. *The Art of Mingling*, a self-help book on overcoming shyness, offers this advice: "I can't stress enough how important the white lie is in mingling, especially when you are faced with imminent disaster of some kind."

White lies have been around for centuries, but one memorable expression for not speaking honestly—"economical with the truth"—became a catchphrase only in 1986. That's when the British cabinet secretary, Robert Armstrong, appeared as a witness in an Australian trial—the British government was trying to prevent *Spycatcher*, a memoir by Peter Wright, a retired UK counterintelligence officer, from being published there. Armstrong was asked if a particular letter contained a lie. He said no, but admitted the letter gave "a misleading impression." Pressed about why a misleading impression was any different from a lie,

Armstrong replied, "It is perhaps being economical with the truth." The idiom soon entered wide use—partly because, unlike a blunt accusation of lying, "economical with the truth" is vague enough to forestall a potential lawsuit.

In the past, a person who swears a lot was said to have a sailor's mouth. Sailors were notorious for using foul language or, as it was sometimes said, "language that would fry bacon"— a clever play on the notion that oaths were hot on the tongue. "Swear like a trooper" and "swear a blue streak" are both American expressions—the blue streak originally meant a bolt of lightning. But the verb *swear* is a kind of double agent: apart from meaning profanity, it also refers to a solemn vow. If you "swear on a stack of Bibles" or "swear on my mother's grave," it's unlikely a blue streak will come into sight. The word *oath* has a similar dual meaning: when it's not a curse, it's a sworn declaration.

Some idioms are unlikely to ever go out of style, and they provide no sign of their age or origin. "Word of mouth," for example, is as current now as it was in the fifteenth century and as it probably will be in the twenty-fifth. But other expressions give an indelible sense of period and place. "Fine words butter no parsnips" is redolent of rural England in past centuries. Those sturdy root vegetables need some extra flavor, and exalted language won't do the trick. In its mistrust of eloquence, the idiom is reminiscent of a better-known proverb, "Actions speak louder than words." "Them's fightin' words" is suggestive of backwoods America a century ago, although the expression can also be dressed up more formally: "Those are fighting words."

It's not just the countryside that breeds idioms, but also the cities where most people now live. One idiom that speaks to our own era is "throw shade." It means to be critical or show contempt, often in a nonverbal way, and it emerged from the gay club scene in New York in the 1980s and 1990s, especially the world of black and Latino drag queens. Shade can be thrown with a smirk, a raised eyebrow, a turning away, a meaningful pause. But it can also involve language. When the *Seattle Times* summed up the consensus opinion of a 2017 movie, its headline read: "Critics Throw Shade at *50 Shades Darker*: It's 'Utterly Ridiculous.'" Throwing shade can blur into another idiom that characterizes the present day: "trash-talking."

Lies, oaths, personal attacks. Does English have no idioms that show a happier view of language?

Spoonfuls of sugar

Proverbial expressions often take the form of warnings: they look to the future with foreboding. Don't be shocked, then, that many proverbs begin with "don't." From looking a gift horse in the mouth to changing horses in midstream, from mixing business with pleasure to casting pearls before swine, and from letting the grass grow under our feet to sweating the small stuff, English is rich in rebukes. Don't forget how U2 sported with all this in their 1993 song "Numb." It featured a long series of spoken commands. Don't run before you can walk, for example. And don't fall down on your sword, either.

Thankfully, it does. Anything that's novel or surprising, for instance, can be a "conversation piece." When a girl in Hamilton, Ontario, found an alligator near her family's backyard swimming pool, her father was reported as saying, "I'm glad no one was hurt . . . When you think back on it, it's a nice little conversation piece." (The residents of Hamilton must be cucumber cool.) If I'm "hanging on your every word," I'm paying close attention and I'm keen to know what you'll say next. Should you be someone I greatly admire, I "won't hear a word against you." I might encourage you by giving you a pep talk, or we could engage in direct and honest communication by means of straight talk.

Agree with something I just said, and you might inform me that I "took the words right out of your mouth." Only if we were surprisingly intimate, though, would we move on to "pillow talk."

Those idioms about language are characteristic of how words can crystallize, clarify, and confuse our thinking on all matter of subjects. Food and drink, love and sex, illness and death, weather and time: all these and more have generated a rich vocabulary of human perception. "We die," the novelist Toni Morrison said when she accepted the Nobel Prize for literature. "That may be the meaning of life. But we do language. That may be the measure of our lives." By focusing on the fragments of language that sum up our feelings and convictions, we can begin to understand larger patterns of thought. Do old idioms still reflect the truth of twenty-first-century lives? Which new expressions deserve to last?

A phrase becomes idiomatic only when it catches a mood or sentiment that has been felt not just by one person but by many. It touches a common nerve, so to speak; it strikes a familiar chord. Idioms are democratic in spirit. We may not always like what they reveal about past history and present beliefs—we may wish they were more tender, less sexist, less militaristic—but "if wishes were horses, beggars would ride." English idioms can be merciless. They puncture many kinds of illusion.

Besides, idioms are central to the music of language. Whether a Top 40 hit or a Mahler symphony, every piece of music is built up of melodies consisting of multiple notes. The ways in which these melodies are repeated, altered and harmonized help to create the overall mood of a piece and affect the impact it has on listeners. Likewise, our verbal acts—from a casual conversation to a poem or a political speech—comprise not just individual words but whole phrases. Idioms are recurrent melodies. Used wisely and creatively, they allow language to sing.

So let's investigate more of these expressions. I invite you to come along for the ride. Even if the journey's end is no laughing matter, getting there will be half the fun.

Swan Dive

ogs are sometimes said to be man's best friend. You wouldn't know it by the way the English language treats them.

When a movie is a dog, it's so bad that nobody in her right mind would want to see it. If a person looks like a dog, a potential sexual partner is unlikely to take much interest. A country is going to the dogs when it's deteriorating fast. A resident of that country would be dogged by misfortune and could be excused for wearing a hangdog expression. Summing up his experience of being shipwrecked alone on a desert island, Robinson Crusoe says, "I was an unfortunate dog."

Granted, there's a constellation known as Canis Major, or the Great Dog, and the brightest star in the sky, Sirius (the Dog Star), belongs to that constellation. It seems like a noble title.

But it would be wrong to see anything positive for dogs in that name. At the hottest time of year, Sirius rises late in the night, and ancient Romans believed that the star drained energy away from human beings. Days of indolence, torpor and high humidity: these were, the Romans believed, the dog days of summer. They were an unproductive time of year, sickly and dangerous.

In its sour tone, the phrase "dog days" is all too typical of the way our language treats domestic animals. The Bible asserts that humans, being made in God's image, enjoy "dominion over the fish of the sea, and over the fowl of the air, and over the cattle, and over all the earth, and over every creeping thing." Some of the fowl, and all of the cattle and creeping things—domestic animals, including dogs—have had a rough time in language ever since.

"You can't teach an old dog new tricks" is a proverb that evokes the aging brains of people, yet dogs are the creatures that it uses to make its point. If you're dogging it at work, you're cheating your employer—but if you spend too long on the job, you'll end up dog-tired. When *Classic Rock* magazine wanted to pour scorn on *The Golden Scarab*, a solo album by Ray Manzarek of the Doors, they didn't just describe it as an ugly mess; they called it "the biggest dog's breakfast in the entire history of the state of California." (You might say that in attempting to reshape his musical career, Manzarek was barking up the wrong tree.)

The dogs of war are vicious, and the dogs of hell are nightmarish. True, the term "watchdog" can have positive associations: major newspapers and broadcasters are often described as the watchdogs of democracy, especially at times when democracy is under threat. But the opposite of a watchdog is a lapdog. Centuries ago, a lapdog was merely a small, furry creature that could easily be petted by its owner. Over time, that image of domesticated loyalty and devotion was twisted and carried to an extreme. Today the word conjures up the picture of a weakling, glad to carry out whatever favors a powerful master demands.

Tomatoes on Your Eyes

In April 2017, after a soccer team's bus was bombed in Germany, police were puzzled by a letter left at the scene of the explosion. As the *Toronto Star* reported, "Experts say the letter's mix of correct, complicated German and obvious mistakes raises the possibility it is a red herring." A deliberate deception, in other words.

Mystery novelists love to mislead their readers by planting false clues. These clues have long been known as "red herrings." It's said that smoked herrings, which can have a reddish color, were used in the past to draw hunting dogs toward or away from a particular scent. But no red herring has ever swum in the sea.

"To lead a dog's life" is to endure a miserable existence, and "to die a dog's death" is to suffer a wretched death. In the English language, one of the few creatures less desirable than a male dog is a female one—a bitch, that is. A thousand years ago, a bitch was nothing more or less than a female dog. But ever since the late Middle Ages, the term has also functioned as a vicious sneer or insult targeting a woman. Hillary Clinton was repeatedly subjected to such attacks during the 2016 presidential campaign in the United States. Anyone who insults a man, of course, can resort to the phrase "son of a bitch."

Perhaps in the future, things could be different. The miserable associations that dogs suffer from in English may be changing for the better. If so, dog lovers can thank the influence of hip-hop. Among black men and boys in America's inner cities, a dog can now be a homie, or a good friend. To say "What's up, dog?" in most of the English-speaking world would still be a risky inquiry. But in parts of Chicago and Los Angeles, it's a sign of affection. The only way for Calvin Cordozar Broadus Jr. to succeed in the realm of LA hip-hop was to rebrand himself—and as Snoop Dogg, he achieved global fame.

If dogs want to improve their reputations, they might look to their age-old enemy: the cat. A couple of generations ago, African American culture helped alter the connotations of "cat." In the jazz world, a cat refers to a person (usually a man) who loves the music or plays it brilliantly. "This Black Cat Has Nine Lives" is the title of a song by the great singer and trumpeter Louis Armstrong. As the song ends, Armstrong utters a gruff, drawn-out "Meow." The word *cat* has been adopted across the industry—to this day, many of the T-shirts, posters, bags and other merchandise sold by the Montreal International Jazz

Festival, one of the largest in the world, feature the image of a cat.

Johnny Mize, a baseball slugger of the Second World War era, was nicknamed "The Big Cat," and a *New York Times* obituary described him as "the hulking Hall of Fame first baseman who moved with feline grace." But the meanings of "feline" aren't always so happy. According to *Webster's New Universal Unabridged Dictionary*, feline also means "sly; cruel; treacherous; crafty; stealthy." "She attracted admirers in slavish droves," reads a sentence in a novel by the best-selling author Wilbur Smith, "and then dropped them with almost feline cruelty." To call someone feline—especially a woman—can be a catty remark. An old name for a brothel was a cathouse. Chances are, a married man caught in a cathouse would immediately find himself in the doghouse—in disgrace, that is.

Combing the Giraffe

Japanese is unusually rich in cat-related idioms, some of them obscure to English speakers. The "cat's forehead," for example, refers to a very small space. If you wear a cat on your head, you're only pretending to be friendly. To appear in a cat veil means to feign innocence. As for throwing a coin before a cat, this phrase has much the same meaning in Japanese as "casting pearls before swine" does in English, with the proviso that cats are valued more highly in Japan than pigs are nearly everywhere on Earth.

A few idioms, admittedly, treat cats with disdain. A child who's anxious or frightened risks being called a scaredy-cat. And if you're trying to decide on a course of action among several options, you might announce "There's more than one way to skin a cat." Still, for the most part, our language does allow cats a certain measure of dignity. "A cat may look at a king" means that everyone has rights, regardless of wealth, power or social status. Idioms that allude to other animals seldom give them access to royalty.

It may be that language preserves a distant memory of cats from ancient Egypt, where they were revered as gods. Without cats' ability to devour crop-eating rodents, the civilization of the Nile would not have blossomed so early. The proverb "When the cat's away, the mice will play" survives as a distant reminder of the critical role cats have played in human history. Today, if you put the cat among the pigeons, you're bent on causing trouble. But maybe everything will go the way you hope, in which case life will prove to be the cat's meow.

English has almost nothing good to say about rodents. "You dirty rat!" and "Are you man or mouse?" are ancient sayings. More recently, "guinea pig" has come to mean the passive subject of an experiment. Rats and mice carried bubonic plague and other diseases, so people had good reason to keep them at a distance. Even today, when you smell a rat, you suspect some kind of treachery. If you pull a rat, you're guilty of treachery yourself.

The phrase "rat race" started off as military slang. In the United

States, after the First World War, it referred to risky maneuvers carried out by ships and planes. Within a few years, though, "rat race" had turned into a metaphor for the drudgery and stress of modern life, especially in large cities, where the riskiest maneuver in many people's lives is their daily commute. Old habits die hard, and rodents can't escape their historical reputation.

By contrast, English idioms show a surprising tolerance, even fondness, for insects. A gregarious person who flits between parties and events is known as a "social butterfly." Wings are also essential to being "a fly on the wall": uncomfortable though it sounds, that position can give you access to privileged news. Greater comfort lies in being "snug as a bug in a rug." The fun of those repeated rhymes outweighs the idea that nobody wants to find insects lurking in the carpet. To the great annoyance of some philosophers, mathematicians and IT specialists, language is never wholly rational.

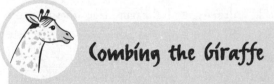

Combing the Giraffe

Ah, the mysteries of Paris! The French language warns its speakers not to look for the little beast, not to comb the giraffe, not to have the cockroach, and not to place a rabbit. What in the name of Napoleon are all these animal idioms saying?

"To go looking for the little beast" is to be always complaining about something small: to be a nitpicker, that is. "To comb the giraffe" means to perform a tedious, useless task. "Having the cockroach" involves suffering from depression, or, as we say in English, having the blues. And "to place a rabbit," surprisingly, is to stand someone up—an English phrase that, when you stop to think about it, doesn't make much sense either.

Rats and mice fare badly in idioms, but so do many of the creatures that feed our bellies. English treats chickens with particular contempt. They're most often a symbol of cowardice. When you're afraid to do something, you might chicken out of it—clear proof that you're chickenhearted. It's a mistake to count your chickens before they're hatched. The result of that sort of overconfidence is obvious when chickens come home to roost: that is, when something from your past returns to haunt you in the present. Among the most gruesome idioms in the language is one for frenzied haste: running around "like a chicken with its head cut off."

Hens are female chickens, and the language doesn't grant them much respect, either. For a man to be henpecked is widely considered shameful. "Hen brained" and "hen headed" are old phrases for stupidity. By contrast, a male chicken—usually called a rooster today—was known as a cock, and cheerful old phrases like "cock of the walk" and "cock-a-hoop" point to a stark contrast in power between males and females. Dogs are by no means the only species in which females are more likely than males to be victimized in metaphors and idioms.

If chickens are a symbol of weakness, turkeys are seen as

failures. Suppose a reviewer of a new movie or play dismisses the work as a turkey. That's just as bad—and means basically the same—as if the reviewer had described the work as a dog. Anyone who calls you a turkey is probably implying that you are, let's say, not playing with a full deck, or that your elevator doesn't reach the top floor, or that you're a few bricks shy of a load. (Speakers of English have fun evoking feeblemindedness.) In US medical schools, "turkey" is a slang word for a patient whose many complaints have no physical origin.

One of the small puzzles of English involves the origin of the modern phrase "cold turkey," meaning a sudden withdrawal from alcohol, drugs or some other addiction. What does that have to do with bulky poultry? A well-known guess connects the appearance of goose bumps with the cold, burning feeling that addicts undergo in the withdrawal process. But the phrase was recorded as long ago as 1910, in a sentence where "cold turkey" simply meant "outright," with no hint of addiction. The expression probably began as a blend of "cold" (hard-headed) and "talk turkey" (speak frankly), and only later came to evoke the avoidance of bottles or needles.

 ## Tomatoes on Your Eyes

Kangaroos do not leap around courtrooms. They do not have trials. They are neither judges nor criminals. So why should a makeshift court with no legal standing—or a real court that uses unfair practices to convict the innocent—go by the name "kangaroo court"?

Nobody knows for sure. The idiom sprang to life not in Australia but in the American West, a region sadly devoid of kangaroos, soon after the California gold rush of the 1840s. One possibility involves the miners who descended on the Wild West having previously searched for gold in Australia—they brought with them a sharp memory of the only large mammal that moves around by hopping. In Australian English, a group of kangaroos has always been known as a mob. And maybe the experience of mob justice in California and Texas provoked some grizzled veterans of Australia to start talking about kangaroo courts.

Other farm animals have also generated a host of idioms. Anybody or anything that annoys you is said to "get your goat." A goat can refer to a fool, or a lecherous old man, or a slow racehorse, or an athlete whose bad play has cost a team the game. That athlete would then "wear the goat's horns." Goats are, at least, not accused of cowardice as sheep are, judging by phrases such as "sheep hearted" and "sheep spirited." A member of any flock that engages in unwise or unsafe actions can be described as a black sheep. When a black sheep goes too far, it's in danger of becoming a lost sheep.

Idioms that mention puppies, kittens, ponies and calves mostly have a gentler tone than expressions involving the grownup members of those species. A young goat or antelope is known as a kid, and for hundreds of years, "kid" referred only to animals. "Two shakes of a lamb's tail" is an old expression for speed, relying on the idea that a frisky lamb moves its tail quickly. "Gentle as a lamb" and "innocent as a lamb" are phrases often applied to children. But the cynical idiom "Might as well be hung for a sheep as for a lamb" implies that the same sad fate awaits creatures of any age.

Perhaps no animal is more abused by language than the harmless, inoffensive pig. As if it's not bad enough to be pigheaded, to live like a pig, or to pig out on food and drink, you can behave like a miserable swine who hogs the attention of everyone around you. Pigs, in many other languages as well as English, evoke gluttony and dirtiness. In Homer's *Odyssey*, composed more than twenty-five hundred years ago, the witch Circe transforms Odysseus's crew into pigs. A worse fate could not be imagined. Maybe it was to redeem the reputation of pigs that J. K. Rowling gave the name Hogwarts to the high school for wizards at the heart of the Harry Potter books. Or maybe Rowling just chose the ugliest name she could dream up. After all, "Hogwarts" is only a few letters removed from "hogwash."

Spoonfuls of sugar

The fantasy of animals doing ridiculous things has led to idioms in several languages that vividly suggest the impossible. In English, we say "when pigs fly" or "when pigs have wings," and some other European languages resort to the same image, among them Norwegian, Welsh and Estonian. But to convey the idea in French, you'd say "when hens have teeth." The Dutch equivalent is "when calves dance on the ice." And Russian takes the idea to a surrealist extreme: "when a lobster whistles on a mountaintop."

Among farm animals, only the bull has earned a grudging measure of consistent respect. Just as the language values male dogs more than bitches and roosters more than hens, it also looks on bulls more kindly than cows. True, the phrase "sacred cow" gives a nod to the Hindu reverence for cattle, but only as a sneer—used as an English idiom, no sacred cow is worth venerating. By contrast, bulls convey a picture of masculine strength. In a bull market, stocks keep on rising. "To have a cow" means to lose self-control in a fit of useless rage, whereas "to seize the bull by the horns" is to take control in a fearless, determined manner. To feel bullish is almost the opposite of feeling cowed.

It's hard to imagine any kind of drink being marketed as "cow's blood," but there's a popular Hungarian red wine known as bull's blood. According to legend, the wine got its name in 1552 when a fortress was under siege. The outnumbered defenders gulped down the local wine and then charged out, yelling at the tops of their voices. When the attackers saw dark red liquid spilling over their enemies' faces and chests, they imagined the defenders had been swallowing the blood of bulls. So they turned tail and ran.

True, there are some risks that come with being bullheaded. But how much worse is it to be chickenhearted?

The scorn that English inflicts on dogs, rodents, poultry and farm animals begins to disappear in what the language says about birds. Not all birds, mind you. Guilt and failure are symbolized by the image of an albatross around the neck. To parrot a sentence is to repeat it without understanding, something you'd want to do only if you were bird-brained. In truth, birds are surprisingly intelligent, none more so than crows and ravens, and a few phrases in our language recognize that. To crow over something suggests that you've enjoyed a success worth celebrating, and if you travel as the crow flies, your route is a straightforward one.

A few well-known idioms about birds emerge from close observation of the natural world. "One swallow doesn't make a summer" implies that it's a mistake to read too much into a single example of anything. The proverb makes sense if you know that, in their haste to find a mate and build a nest, the first swallows sometimes return too soon from their winter migration, when late frosts and snowfalls can kill them off. "Birds of a feather flock together" comes from the recognition that while species as different as ducks, sandpipers and pelicans migrate in groups, those groups always remain separate. In human terms, the phrase implies that people with similar backgrounds and tastes prefer one another's company.

Thanks to their size, physical grace and purity of color, swans are among the most impressive of all birds. A "swan dive" is an elegant act that requires a diver to enter water with the arms stretched above the head. The expression "swan song" began in a legend—that on the threshold of death, a normally silent swan would burst into glorious song—and became an idiom for any experience nearing its end. Through most of European history, swans were white by definition: the Roman poet Juvenal used the image of black swans to symbolize the impossible. But when European sailors reached Australia, they found black swans in abundance. In the twenty-first century, the financial analyst and author Nassim Nicholas Taleb coined the expression "black swan event" to mean unexpected discoveries and events that become explicable, even predictable, only because we concoct after-the-fact explanations.

Other, less impressive types of fowl, such as geese and ducks, don't share the esteem bestowed on swans. If you're a lame duck, you have no power; if you're a silly goose, you're unusually foolish. You'd better smarten up, or you might soon be a dead duck. An ugly duckling is someone who in the realm of myth—but not so often in real life—turns into a swan, the epitome of beauty. And the expression "All his geese are swans" applies to a person who exaggerates wildly and fails to recognize the truth. It's as if we aspire to be swans, an aspiration not borne out by life.

Some common words and expressions don't reveal their origin easily. The proverb "A bird in the hand is worth two in the bush" comes from the ancient sport of falconry. The bird in hand was a falcon, rare and highly trained, while the birds in the bush were whatever falcons might hunt. It's clear which one was more valuable. In its caution against risk, the proverb stands in opposition to an equally familiar idiom: "Nothing ventured, nothing gained." (No one ever accused the English language of consistency.) Falconry also gave us the adjective "haggard." In the sixteenth century, a hawk that was captured after attaining its adult plumage was said to be haggard, or wild-looking and untamed. Over time, people adopted the word for themselves, and "haggard" became a term applied to rough-looking or distraught human beings.

Falcons are birds of prey, and birds of prey have always earned respect in language. To watch somebody like a hawk is to keep a very close eye on them. An "eagle eye" perspective brings clarity to a broad picture. In golf, a birdie is good—but an eagle is even better. As the national bird of the United States, the bald eagle has become, in some quarters, a fierce symbol of liberty. "You won't mind a body bragging a little about his country on the Fourth of July," the American novelist Mark Twain once wrote. "It is a fair and legitimate time to fly the eagle."

The British equivalent to the bald eagle is the lion, a mammal once nicknamed "the king of beasts." In the heyday of the British Empire, any foreigner who dared defy Queen Victoria's government was said to "twist the lion's tail." But whereas bald eagles in popular culture are inevitably tied to Washington, lions are not restricted to London. Hollywood's witty adaptation of *Hamlet* into an animated animal movie was entitled *The Lion King*, yet the evil Scar (voiced by Jeremy Irons) was the only mammal with a British accent. When anything gets divided up, "the lion's share" refers to the largest portion. Some years, the month of March is said to come in like a lion (with storms and rough weather) and go out like a lamb (in the sunlight of early spring).

Predators and sex make a linguistically alluring mix. Sexually powerful men can be described as wolves. Wolves often howl; men occasionally "wolf whistle." In gay culture, a bear is a burly man with lots of body hair. Women who enjoy sexual relationships with younger men are cougars, and a good-looking woman is sometimes called a fox. In the eyes of men like Harvey Weinstein, any attractive woman is consigned to the role of sex kitten, fox or cougar.

Household Names

If you're choosing a name for a new sports team, look for animals that devour other animals. Major-league teams in North American baseball, football, basketball and hockey are rife with examples. The Timberwolves and the Coyotes. The Grizzlies, the Bruins and the Bears. The Lions, the Jaguars, the Panthers and the Tigers. The Eagles, the Hawks, the Falcons and the Raptors.

We can add a few smaller birds to the list: Blue Jays, Cardinals, Orioles. And in the lower depths of minor-league baseball, less heralded animals emerge: the Southern Maryland Blue Crabs, the Greensboro Grasshoppers, the Idaho Falls Chukars, and so on. (A chukar is a small striped partridge, much hunted around Idaho Falls.)

But the names of major-league teams need greater force and fury than you can obtain from grasshoppers, chukars, or crabs of any color. In the 2016 National Hockey League playoffs, the San Jose Sharks battled the Nashville Predators. Now try to imagine the San Jose Minnows facing off against the Nashville Herbivores.

What we admire, it seems, are other creatures at the top of the food chain—or creatures even bigger than ourselves. Today a "white elephant" refers to any grossly expensive and futile pursuit. But white elephants aren't what they used to be. For centuries, the king of Siam—what we now call Thailand—prided himself on keeping a small number of unusually pale elephants. These animals appear in both Hindu and Buddhist mythology, and they had to be well cared for. It's said that the expense of keeping white elephants was so great that if the king gave one to a courtier, the recipient would be financially ruined. We may have forgotten this odd sliver of history but, as the saying goes, "An elephant never forgets."

Advertising agencies have often turned to big predators in quest of memorable phrases and images. Think of the names of cars: Jaguar and Barracuda, Stingray and Cobra, Thunderbird and Bobcat. (Volkswagen bucked the trend with the Beetle and, later, the Rabbit.) One of Esso's most popular slogans, going back to 1959, was "Put a tiger in your tank." A generation later, a writer for a Catholic newspaper in New Zealand found the slogan helpful for other purposes: "Young girls must be made to realize that boys of the same age have a 'tiger in their tank' as far as sexual desire goes." People or nations who are weaker than they like to think are sometimes called "paper tigers," a Chinese expression made famous by the Communist leader Mao Zedong. "All reactionaries are paper tigers," he claimed. In popular culture, paperless tigers embody power, speed, courage—and savagery too.

It Is Written

Any time you speak of "a fly in the ointment" (a problem or flaw) or "a nest of vipers" (a group of evil-minded people), you're using an expression that sprang to life in the Bible. Indeed the Bible is full of animals, though not always the obvious ones. Cats, which were worshipped in ancient Egypt, are mentioned there only once. Instead we find mythical dragons, satyrs, griffons, behemoths, and the strange, terrifying Leviathan—a landlubber's nightmare of a great whale.

Jesus used one of the most memorable idioms in the Bible to suggest that money is the root of much evil. He declared, "It is easier for a camel to go through the eye of a needle, than for a rich man to enter into the kingdom of God." The British writer Evelyn Waugh quoted this remark in his novel *Brideshead Revisited*, where the fabulously wealthy Lady Marchmain explains it away by saying: "Animals are always doing the oddest things in the lives of the saints."

The human psyche has long been gripped by images of creatures we cannot tame or control. Alexander the Great, whose forces conquered much of Asia twenty-four hundred years ago, is said to have declared, "An army of sheep led by a lion is superior to an army of lions led by a sheep." Some versions of the proverb replace the sheep by stags, but the meaning remains the same. In ancient Rome, to be in a risky position was known as "holding a wolf by the ears." And in the English language for the past five centuries, anyone showing insincere grief has been shedding "crocodile tears."

Of all the carnivorous animals in the world, sharks fare the worst in language. A shark can mean a swindler, a greedy landlord, a lawyer or a merciless usurer—a "loan shark," that is. Sharks feed on fish that could otherwise go into the mouths of people: Is that why English gives them such a bad rap? Perhaps, but many species of whale do the same, and to have "a whale of a time" is to be unusually happy.

Images and idioms surrounding predators and, indeed, all large wild animals suggest a curious mix of human emotions. They are dangerous and also worthy of esteem; they are merciless and also intelligent. In short, they remind us of ourselves. Watch out for a bear with a sore head. And don't let a fox guard the henhouse— anyone who's crazy like a fox is not really crazy at all.

But the ever-widening gap between human society and the natural world has left many idioms orphaned, so to speak. To talk about "making a beeline" or "leading a horse to water" can seem nostalgic, even quaint. In their place, abstract modern terms like "ecosystem management" and "environmental resource" only cut us off further from nature. The English author George Monbiot, writing in the *Guardian* in August 2017, asked: "If Moses had promised the Israelites a land flowing with mammary secretions and insect vomit, would they have followed him into Canaan? Though this means milk and honey, I doubt it would have inspired them. So why do we use such language to describe the natural wonders of the world?" Idiomatic language is not guilty of abstraction—it retains vigor and vibrancy.

The profusion of animal-related idioms shows how crucial animals once were in the human realm. Rural life was inconceivable without them. As society has grown more urban, animals have become less visible. But they remain central to our imagination. Children don't cuddle stuffed plants or stuffed machines—they play with, and cherish, stuffed animals. Their nursery rhymes are full of black sheep, climbing spiders, courting frogs, king's horses, wandering geese, jumping cows, violin-playing cats, and weasel-chasing monkeys.

But children do tend to grow up. And as we've seen, the language spoken by adults shows little respect for many animals. If, as some still believe, humans are the only living beings with souls and all other creatures were put on this planet for our benefit, then we're free to abuse them as we please. As we did. As, on factory farms, we still do. It would be pleasant to think we're becoming more enlightened. But if so, our words and idioms have yet to catch up with our understanding.

Beefcake

The English language looks on hunger as an animal—a ruthless, predatory animal. It's no accident that Little Red Riding Hood is gobbled up by a famished wolf, for wolves can be the embodiment of hunger. "A growing boy has a wolf in his belly," we say, or "I'm trying to keep the wolf from the door," or simply "I'm hungry as a wolf." We don't say "I could eat a wolf," although we do invoke other large and unlikely mammals to express the scale of our hunger: "I could eat a horse," an ox, a bear, or even an elephant.

And if the food doesn't taste so good? No problem, for "Hunger is the best sauce." To see the sheer power of hunger and the desperation it provokes, look no further than the title of three of the best-selling novels in recent years: *The Hunger Games* trilogy.

"Death games" might be a more accurate title, considering the hazards faced by the young competitors, but the author, Suzanne Collins, knew exactly what she was doing. Collins is a familiar Irish name, and the terrible famine that swept over Ireland in the mid-nineteenth century, killing more than a million people, is known as the Great Hunger.

Flash forward to the present and, as some people like to say, "My stomach is on E." E for empty, that is.

Once we've eaten our fill—once we've wolfed down our food—we might say we're stuffed to the gills. This is harder to visualize, but also less unpleasant to imagine, than common alternatives such as "stuffed like a turkey" and "stuffed to bursting." Most birds are a tiny fraction of the size of turkeys, which may explain why if you eat like a bird, you merely peck at your food. That phrase is almost the opposite of "eating someone out of house and home," a picture of unrestrained gluttony.

Eating is a rich source of metaphors and idioms, and many of them have nothing to do with the actual food on our plates. To "eat away" at something, for example, means to erode or corrode it. Climate change is likely to mean major losses for Florida, the *New York Times* reported in June 2017, as heat waves flare up "and rising sea levels eat away at valuable coastal properties." If I promise to eat my hat if something happens, I'm staking my reputation that it never will. But when you have me "eating out of your hand," I'll do whatever you ask.

Some idioms about hunger are more ambiguous. Their meaning changes according to the tone of voice and the relationship between the speaker and the person being addressed. Suppose a friend says to you, "I made a fantastic beef Wellington last night—eat your heart out, Jamie Oliver!" You know right away that your friend is making no great claims about his ability in the kitchen. But what if your friend lowers his voice and confides, "My mother's Alzheimer's is getting worse. It's eating my heart out"? The same phrase can embody both light banter and heart-felt grief.

The idiom has an ancient origin, and a deeply somber one. Nearly three thousand years ago, the Greek poet Homer imagined the hero Bellerophon wandering alone on a desolate plain and gnawing at his own heart after the gods killed two of his children. Bellerophon couldn't stomach his loss; he found it impossible to swallow.

For hundreds of years, "eat your heart out" referred only to grief. Its rebirth as a phrase of humorous envy took place in modern America, the graveyard of much solemnity. Many curses and oaths have undergone a similar loss of gravity—"Damn you" and "I swear by high heaven" were once expressions of the utmost seriousness.

Combing the Giraffe

When we're searching for a colorful way to evoke hesitation, caution or long-windedness, we might say "beat around the bush"—an expression that comes from bird-hunting. Some of the people in-volved, instead of aiming weapons, would thrash away in the vegeta-tion, eventually allowing others to capture or kill the birds that flew out. The Czech and Slovak languages of central Europe express the same idea by saying "walk around hot porridge." Scandinavians make the idea even more graphic—in Norwegian and Finnish, you "walk around hot porridge like a cat."

Plenty of other phrases involve the act of swallowing. If you "swallow your pride," or your principles, you're agreeing to do something even though it makes you feel bad. That kind of action is "a bitter pill to swallow"—it's unpleasant, but it needs to be done. If you believe something that later proves to be a lie, you've "swallowed it hook, line and sinker," a graphic image from fishing. And if you feel truly terrible as a result, you may "wish the ground would swallow you up." Time and again, the English language tells us that we need to be very careful what we take inside ourselves.

People who have tried to reach a goal that proves to be beyond their abilities are said to have "bitten off more than they can chew." As with swallowing, both biting and chewing are used in a range of idioms. If you "chew someone out," for example, you're delivering a severe reprimand. But if you "chew something over," you're thinking hard. To "bite the hand that feeds you" is to be seriously ungrateful; to "bite someone's head off" is to show that person just how angry you are. To bite the dust (or bite the big one) is, quite simply, to die. Biting is among the more common verbs in English idioms, and most of the meanings involve suffering.

If you bite something slowly and continually, you're "gnawing away" at it. Gnawing suggests a slow, continual pain or hunger. A biting pain is sharper and more sudden.

For those who have no other weapons, teeth can always suffice.

I suppose it's remotely possible that all those idioms for eating, biting and chewing have done a little to "make your mouth water" or "whet your appetite" (sharpen it, that is to say). Or they may have "wet your whistle" (left you thirsty, I mean). For as soon as we've got beyond the threat of hunger, our thoughts often turn to drink. And no, I don't mean milk. Or water, either. To quote the American comedian W. C. Fields: "Once, during Prohibition, I was forced to live on nothing but food and water."

Throughout history, alcohol has been the source of much pleasure as well as much bad and dangerous behavior, and English reflects our long fascination with what temperance movements liked to call "the demon drink." Among the countless euphemisms for being drunk is "under the influence." The phrase stops there; nobody needs to explain what influence is meant. Likewise, nobody needs to ask what you can buy at a "thirst-aid station." But there are plenty of other idioms that do require some explanation.

A Canadian expression for a man's protruding belly,

"Molson muscle," features the name of one of the country's largest brewers (the company is said to make "barley sandwiches," a fine metaphor for beer). The British speak of a drunk person as "tired and emotional," a euphemism that was often applied to deputy prime minister George Brown in the late 1960s, a time when the media were more deferential than they are today. But only in Australia would you hear drunkenness referred to as "Adrian Quist."

Why? The real Adrian Quist, a native of South Australia, was a tennis star. He ranked among the best doubles players in the world in the 1930s and 1940s, winning two Wimbledon titles and a US Open. *Life* magazine once described him as "a dark, short, chipmunk of a man." What does all this have to do with overimbibing? Well, the Australians took from their Cockney forebears a fondness for rhyming slang—"apples and pears," for "stairs," is a good example—and in Britain and Australia alike, a common synonym for drunk is "pissed." The chipmunk-resembling Quist was unlucky enough to have a family name that made a perfect rhyme for that word, and it stuck. The English went with the loftier "Brahms and Liszt" to describe their own overindulgence.

Australians also have an expression for extreme thirst that you might not want to use in polite company: "dry as a dead dingo's donger."

Combing the Giraffe

What is it about carrots? Why do crunchy orange vegetables show up in so many idioms? In English, if we want to invoke a balance between reward and punishment, we might talk about a "carrot-and-stick approach." (Swallow the carrot, please, or else you'll feel the weight of this heavy stick across your shoulders.) In French, "The carrots are cooked" means the game is over, and it's too late to make a change. An old British expression, "The goose is cooked," gets a similar point across. You can't always restore things to their original state.

That's clear? Then you'll appreciate the simple Korean expression "It's a carrot!" Of course (so the meaning goes), it's obvious! The German idiom "scrub the carrot" is no mystery: it means to masturbate. But I'm not sure why the Dutch say "I'm sweating little carrots" to express what, in English, we refer to as sweating like a pig. And if that's not blatant enough for you, try the slang expression for vomit in Hungarian: "cubes of carrot."

Anywhere in the English-speaking world, a person who has had too much to drink can be described as "three sheets to the wind." This is a nautical idiom whose long and murky history goes back to the big sailing ships of the early nineteenth century. On those ships, a sheet was not a sail but a rope, one of several that held the sail in place. If a sailor was one sheet in the wind ("in" being the original preposition), he'd drunk a fair quantity of rum. Two sheets in the wind, and he'd drunk a little too much. Three sheets in the wind meant he was at risk of toppling overboard.

More recent idioms for the same behavior include "pie-faced" and "walleyed," both calling out the physical appearance of a drunken person, and "drunk as a lord," referring to the aristocracy's tendency to go over the top. In Britain, that phrase overtook and eventually silenced the earlier "drunk as a beggar." In North America, people are more likely to say "drunk as a skunk," maybe because of the rhyme, or maybe because of the unpleasant results of a chance meeting.

The release of inhibitions makes prime fodder for comedy, and from *Beerfest* to *Sideways*, *House Party* to *The Hangover*, Hollywood knows that audiences love to laugh at other people's drinking. But the English language got there first. In the spontaneity and off-the-wall humor of these and many other idioms about alcohol, the language mimics the relaxing effect of the drink itself. The same is true for expressions about smoking marijuana: "flying Mexican Airlines," "clam baking," "hot boxing," "having a green day" and more.

Back to food. Or, we would have said in the past, back to meat. The word *meat* once referred to any solid food, not just the flesh of dead animals. In a few phrases, it still carries that older meaning. If you want to remind a listener that people are allowed to have very different beliefs, you could say: "One man's meat is another man's poison." The expression "meat and drink" still survives, and occasionally you might hear the old term "sweet-meat" to mean dessert.

Merchant of Words

"A dish fit for the gods" conjures up the ancient Greek idea of ambrosia, a food reserved for the immortals on Mount Olympus. But the expression was invented by William Shakespeare, and in his play *Julius Caesar*, the context for the phrase is unlike anything you might expect. It appears when Marcus Brutus and some of Rome's leading senators are plotting to assassinate Caesar, an ambitious general who has become a dictator. "Gentle friends," Brutus says, "Let's kill him boldly, but not wrathfully; / Let's carve him as a dish fit for the gods." It's not exactly taramasalata.

"The milk of human kindness" has an equally surprising source. Lady Macbeth, one of Shakespeare's great villains, says of her husband, "Yet do I fear thy nature. / It is too full o' the milk of human kindness." Macbeth goes on to kill or order the murder of the king of Scotland, the king's two guards, his rival's wife, his rival's children, his rival's wife's servants, the teenage son of an English general, and his own best friend. The milk of human kindness evidently curdled.

Much as I might want the English language to show vegetarian sympathies, it doesn't. Many of its idioms have a carnivorous feel, as if the most significant element of meat (all kinds of food) was meat (dead flesh). To make meat of a proposal is to kill it, whereas to be dead meat is to face the prospect of serious punishment. "Meat and two veg" suggests something that is standard, typical or unimaginative (it can also refer to male genitalia). It's a British idiom, not too far removed from the American "meat and potatoes"—a *Rolling Stone* journalist once noted, "Vocal harmonies are the meat and potatoes of California's pop identity." As for "red meat," the phrase has come to refer to a kind of vicious, ill-informed rhetoric, full of hatred, that's now all too prevalent on talk radio and grisly internet sites.

Particular meats have attracted their own idioms. In much the same way that English treats pigs with contempt, it also looks unkindly on pork. "Pork-barrel politicians" are those who lavish money on expensive projects so as to get reelected. When you've "porked out," you've gorged on too much food. In Britain, "pork pie"—apart from referring to a flat-topped, high-brimmed hat— is rhyming slang for a lie.

Once you alter the nature of pork by salting and curing it, it turns into bacon, at which point it fares much better in English idioms. To "bring home the bacon" is to earn a salary or, more generally, to succeed at a given task. To "save your bacon" is to preserve your own skin, even if others do not. Beef also commands a certain respect in English, despite the common usage of "a beef" to mean a problem. To say "Where's the beef?" is to ask about the substance of something, as opposed to the mere appearance (the phrase took off as a slogan for the Wendy's fast-food chain, aiming to suggest that their competitors' bulked-up hamburgers consisted mostly of oversized buns). "Beefing up" means adding strength or weight, and "beefcake" is slang for a muscular, good-looking man.

Spoonfuls of sugar

A Welsh rabbit is a meatless dish of cooked cheese on toast, sometimes made with diced onions, beer and other seasonings. Many people call it "Welsh rarebit," which makes a certain sense. But "rabbit" is the original form. The idiom probably began as an English sneer: the Welsh, who were seen as unreliable if not inferior, were famously fond of cheese. If you were a family too poor to buy even a cheap cut of meat, "Welsh rabbit" would have to suffice.

English is unusual among languages in that its words for the meat of pigs, cows and sheep are different from the actual names of those animals. After the Norman French conquered England in 1066, the peasants went on eating their modest fare. Apart from the occasional squirrel, their diet contained little meat. It was mainly the aristocratic newcomers who could afford to dine on *porc*, *boeuf* and *mouton*. Over many generations, these French words for animals became the English names for their flesh. Mutton is a rare item on restaurant menus today, but it survives in the saying "mutton dressed as lamb," a cruel phrase often applied to middle-aged women who are trying to look young. The main character in *The Summer Before the Dark*, a novel by Nobel Prize–winning author Doris Lessing, is described as "tinting her hair, keeping her weight down, following the fashions carefully so that she would be smart but not mutton dressed as lamb."

There's a pattern here. Beef does much better in the English language than cows; mutton is the subject of fewer barbs than sheep; bacon receives kinder treatment than pigs. Once we separate the food product from its four-legged, warm-blooded source, we're less likely to treat it with scorn.

"Hard-headed bird don't make good soup," says a Caribbean idiom for stubbornness. A "pea-souper" is the name for the thick fog that often afflicted London when most of its residents burned coal to heat their homes; the vegetables in question were not fresh green peas but dried split ones that gave the soup a brownish-yellow color, just like the polluted air. Soups and stews are often seen as comfort foods. But being "in the soup" is a synonym for trouble. And when we're "stewing over" a problem, it's worrying us a lot. For expressions of comfort and consolation— assuming we don't want to end up three sheets to the wind—we turn to baked goods.

Those idioms, like the breads, cookies and cakes themselves, start off with dough. For nearly two hundred years, dough has been a synonym for money. Anyone who's "rolling in dough" has, to adopt a newer piece of slang, plenty of "bread." "In thirty days, when the loans began to close, I would be rolling in dough again," Jordan Belfort wrote in his memoir *Catching the Wolf of Wall Street*. Belfort found getting rich to be as easy as pie, a somewhat odd expression, given how tricky pies are to bake. But something about pies brings on a rush of hope. Is it the combination of motherhood and apple pie? Or is it the wish to have a finger in every pie? Ultimately, such an ambition is "pie in the sky"—desirable yet unattainable.

Because bread has always been so central to European and North American diets, it features in a host of idioms. Someone whose bread is buttered on both sides is benefiting or profiting from two incompatible sources—a public servant, say, who's taking bribes on the side. "Break bread with" is a Biblical idiom that can be used as a symbol of friendship. The "greatest thing since sliced bread" means anything terrific. And if some experience or product isn't so amazing, but is still acceptable, "half a loaf is better than none."

There's an equal spirit of resignation in the phrase "That's the way the cookie crumbles." In other words, don't be upset. Cookies, like pies, are the mouth-melting objects of childhood desire—hence the notion of getting caught with your hand in the cookie jar. It's difficult to imagine raiding the turnip jar. Of course, adults are the people whose misbehavior in business or politics generally leads to a cookie jar being referenced in the first place—often it's out of their hunger for dough—just as it's usually adults who are complimented on being a tough cookie, a sharp cookie or a smart cookie. Praise is sweet indeed.

Donkey's Hind Leg

We consume many of the foods that people ate in the distant past, and we use many of the same words to describe those foods. As a result, we repeat idioms that emerged, decades or centuries ago, when those food-related words served to make pointed statements about human life. Trouble is, we've forgotten the context that gave birth to some of those idioms, so now they bewilder us.

Think of the common expression "The proof is in the pudding." It doesn't really say much. Admittedly it might be useful as an answer to the question "How much sugar did you put in the dessert?" But the current proverb is actually a shortened form of an older saying that made a lot more sense. Back in the seventeenth century, people would say: "The proof of the pudding is in the eating." Here "proof" has its old meaning of "test," as it still does today in the word *proofread*. You assess the quality of a food not by looking at it but by tasting it. The proverb suggests that appearances may be deceiving—it's best to delay judgment until you know the facts.

English loves cakes almost as much as cookies and pies—if what you do is easy as pie, it's also a piece of cake. When things have gone well, a final piece of good news will be merely the icing on the cake. Of course "You can't have your cake and eat it, too": so says an English proverb, one that often confounds children. (The meaning would be much more obvious if "have" was replaced by "save.") It's an evocative though slightly baffling way of saying we can't always have the best of both worlds. A raunchier equivalent comes from Italian: "You can't have a full wine barrel and a drunken wife."

In the realm of business, a new product that succeeds in the marketplace is said to be "selling like hotcakes." The Shakespearean phrase "cakes and ale" has become symbolic of good times, of fun and pleasure generally (it goes back to the comedy *Twelfth Night*, in which a rowdy courtier named Sir Toby Belch asks a buttoned-up steward, "Dost thou think, because thou art virtuous, / There shall be no more cakes and ale?"). Idioms that mention our beloved baked goods are almost all positive, as though the comfort we take in satisfying our sweet tooth affects the words we utter when we finish chewing.

One of the rare exceptions is an idiom for madness: "fruit cake." Why? Well, fruit cakes are loaded with nuts. The expression relies on the hidden joke.

When a speaker mixes up a pair of idioms, the result can be unintentionally funny. In 2003, for instance, a center for the Indiana Pacers, Brad Miller, tried to explain to reporters why his team was struggling. "It's not going to be peaches and gravy all the time," he said. Was he looking forward to dinner?

Even outside the basketball stadium, idioms involving fruit show a tremendous variety. We can talk about a person having a peaches-and-cream complexion, about blowing a raspberry, about hearing something on the grapevine. "Pear-shaped" is a newer expression for a state of failure or collapse. Lemons have terrific flavor and are rich in vitamin C, but they're most famous for their sourness, and for more than a century, a disappointing or defective product has been called a lemon. The consumer protection laws that exist today—in particular, the ones affecting cars—are widely known as "lemon laws."

But in many languages, including this one, most fruit-related idioms refer to the apple. Perhaps the Bible is responsible. Many people have thought that Adam and Eve were tricked by a serpent into eating an apple. But were they? In the third chapter of Genesis, the identity of the tree of the knowledge of good and evil remains unspecified. The offending plant could have been an apricot tree, a date palm or a fig tree (after all, the guilty couple cover up their nudity with fig leaves). So why have storytellers and preachers, painters and sculptors, always imagined the first two humans crunching into an apple?

The answer is a Roman pun. *Malus* is the Latin word for both apple and evil. And through nearly all its long history, Latin was the essential language of the Roman Catholic Church. By eating an apple, Adam and Eve are said to have brought evil into the world: a crunchy *malus* led to further *malus*. To this day, the bulge in a man's larynx is known as an "Adam's apple" because the forbidden fruit supposedly got stuck in a male throat. By the sexist logic of history, the absence of a similar bulge in a woman's throat showed that women had less trouble swallowing evil.

Some people would say that comparing men and women is like "comparing apples and oranges." From an orange's inedible rind to an apple's unpleasant core, the fruit have a host of obvious differences, and so a comparison between the two seems unfair. Yet in some European languages, the word for orange means "apple from China," while in others, an orange is literally a "golden apple." It's as if apples are the default fruit of many languages, the fruit from which everything else derives or departs.

To make things even more confusing, the Italian word for tomato, *pomodoro*, also means "golden apple." Tomatoes are native to Central and South America. Like squash, pumpkins, potatoes and other vegetables, they entered the mouths of Europeans only after the Spaniards' invasion of what they saw as the New World. The word *tomato* is derived from *tomatl* in the Nahuatl language, spoken throughout the Aztec Empire. But Aztec tomatoes were more likely to be small and yellow than large and red—the absence of flavor in today's supermarket product is a result of commercial breeding to make ripe tomatoes uniformly red.

It took a long time for the word to gain a firm hold in English. For generations, tomatoes were better known as "apples of love." In his *Gardener's Text-book*, published in 1851, the American author Peter Adam Schenck noted that "The well-known tomato, which is now highly esteemed in all kitchens, was formerly raised in the flower garden under the name of love apple." Tomatoes were believed to inspire lust: those juicy apples of love were the crimson Viagra of their day.

Tomatoes on Your Eyes

Food can lead language in weird directions. In German, "to have tomatoes on your eyes" indicates you're missing something obvious. The Portuguese expression "feeding sponge cake to the donkey" refers to giving special treatment to a person who doesn't need it. If you're speaking Hungarian, and you're uncertain if a product is really as good as it's made out to be, you'd say "the fence is not made from sausage." And just across the border, in Romania, it's unwise to "take someone out of his watermelons." It means to drive that person crazy. Or, as we say in English, to drive him nuts.

The health benefits of apples are the basis of the maxim "An apple a day keeps the doctor away." On its first recorded publication, in nineteenth-century Wales, the rhyme was a little different and the financial implications were more specific: "Eat an apple on going to bed, / And you'll keep the doctor from earning his bread." Knowledge of orchards lies behind another proverb, "The apple never falls far from the tree," that transforms a trait of ripe apples into a comment on the behavior of sons and daughters.

Judging by the evidence of language, no country has taken apples to its heart more than the United States. "As American as apple pie" is a well-known figure of speech. One of the country's folk heroes is Johnny Appleseed, who is said to have walked across much of America spreading apples as he went. In fact, the man's name was John Chapman, and he introduced apple-growing in a total of six states by establishing fruit nurseries. Stories, like idioms, thrive on exaggeration.

If you're the sunshine of my life, Stevie Wonder knew, you're also the apple of my eye. That's not a uniquely American ex-pression. It goes back, way back, to a time when the pupil was believed to be a solid sphere inside the eye. In his influential translation of Homer's *Iliad*, the English poet George Chapman described the death of a Trojan soldier by saying: "The dart did undergore his eyelid, by his eye's dear roots, and out the apple fell." After the anatomical error behind this literal meaning was forgotten, the phrase acquired a joyful metaphorical sense. Ap-ples shine brightly and taste sweet: count yourself lucky if you're the apple of somebody's eye.

True, a few idioms use apples to leave a negative impression. A contemptible person can be called a "rotten apple" or a "bad apple." Just as black people who make strenuous efforts to fit into mainstream society are sometimes derided as Oreos—black on the outside, white within—so too indigenous people have been referred to as apples if they only seem red on the outside. And to quote an English saying that has passed from common usage, "He that will not a wife wed, / Must eat a cold apple when he goes to bed."

Donkey's Hind Leg

"Upsetting the apple cart" made perfect sense as an idiom for creating havoc in an age when apples were routinely transported by wheelbarrow. And before fruit could be stored in large refrigerated containers, "one bad apple spoils the barrel" was a superb image for how a single individual can destroy the harmony of a group. We still understand the symbolic meaning of these phrases even though apple carts and barrels are beyond most people's experience.

That's also true for the idiom "extend an olive branch." The literal sense goes back to ancient Greece, where olives were familiar and valuable trees. They were sacred to Athena, the goddess of wisdom, and were widely believed to drive away evil spirits. But people use the phrase now in a very different way. "Justin Trudeau Extends Olive Branch to Indigenous People," said a Vancouver newspaper in August 2017. In symbolic terms, an olive branch is the opposite of a hatchet—and a hatchet can cut an olive tree down.

In our own time, *apple* is not only—not even mainly—a word for a particular fruit. Now it's the name of an iconic technology firm. The legendary cofounder of Apple, Steve Jobs, adopted a fruitarian diet from time to time, and as a young man, he would occasionally leave his home in the San Francisco area to go work in an orchard in Oregon. After one such trip, he gave his new company its name. As he later confided, he was looking for a term that would be "fun, spirited, and not intimidating." He also wanted a name that would come before Atari in the telephone book (a vanishing concept in the twenty-first century, thanks in part to the triumphs of Apple).

That was in 1976. Three years later, another of Apple's early managers, Jef Raskin, was developing a project for a new personal computer. He named it after his favorite kind of apple, one that had first been grown in Canada: the McIntosh. For legal reasons, the company adopted the spelling "Macintosh." Today's MacBooks are direct descendants.

An ancient British idiom declared that any item in ready supply was "as common as blackberries." The phrase arose in a rural society where everyone recognized the wild blackberries growing freely in hedgerows and lanes. But in the urban, technological Britain of the twenty-first century, that idiom has all but disappeared. Perhaps the phrase "as common as Apple" will take its place.

For a time, one of Apple's main competitors was BlackBerry. Until 1998, the prototypes for its email pagers had been known within Research in Motion, the parent company, as PocketLink or MegaMail. But a California branding firm came up with the image of a small, sweet fruit, and (against the wishes of some engineers within the company) BlackBerry was born. Similarly, one of Europe's largest telecommunications companies went by the name Microtel until 1994, when it was rebranded as Orange. More recently, after the Bank of Nova Scotia acquired a Dutch-based electronic bank named ING Direct, they wanted to give their newly purchased firm a fresh identity. ING had used an orange color in its advertising, but "Orange" was now unavailable, so the relaunched bank became Tangerine.

It's revealing that these high-tech corporations have chosen to be identified by something as high-touch and low-tech as fruit. In the business world, image is of prime importance, and what could be more useful in quelling the hunger of consumers than pictures of apples, blackberries, oranges and tangerines? At a time when the green world is under siege in many countries, words and idioms from nature take on a heightened significance. "A rose by any other name would smell as sweet," the young heroine argues in Shakespeare's *Romeo and Juliet*. But the fate of ING Direct, Microtel, PocketLink and MegaMail suggests otherwise.

Serving Time

Many of us are fascinated by the workings of time, even though we tend to complain about how it is treating us. The subjective nature of our experience means that one day, or one year, we feel that time is moving absurdly slowly; a day earlier, or a year later, it moves ridiculously fast. As time goes by, we don't always stand on solid ground. English idioms reveal people's attitudes to the stages of our lives and the passage of time in a multitude of ways.

Let's start with infancy. Some idioms need no explanation—"as smooth as a baby's bottom" and "crybaby," for instance. "Sleep like a baby" is more surprising, because infants don't sleep through the night in their first weeks of life (and a few never do). Sleeping like a baby is an aspiration, not a description. "Taking candy from a baby" is a little perplexing: it would be a very careless parent who gave candy to an infant. But in fact, the phrase is all about power and control; it refers to any action the speaker finds easy.

What about "Don't throw the baby out with the bathwater"? This proverb tells us to hold on to what's essential while getting rid of other things that don't matter. You might come across explanations claiming that, in the past, most families could afford just a single warm bath per day. People would climb into the tub in descending order of age, the water growing cooler and dirtier as everybody took their turn, with the baby coming last of all. Parents supposedly had to be careful when tossing away the grimy water in case the blackened baby fell out, too.

Not quite. The phrase began life in a German satire published in 1512, and it was meant to be outlandish from the start. It became a proverb in Germany, and the Scottish author Thomas Carlyle imported it into English in the mid-nineteenth century. Before then, regardless of their hygiene habits and the size of their family, nobody in the English-speaking world ever worried about discarding a wet baby by accident. Today the proverb is used in a host of contexts, sometimes with unfortunate effect. In October 2017, for instance, a *Financial Times* columnist defended the practice of passing a family business on to a son or daughter by saying, "Throwing out the baby could also be rash. What looks like bath water could in fact be a cocktail of important family traits that gives the business its competitive advantage." Has anyone ever confused bathwater with a cocktail?

It Is Written

"Spare the rod and spoil the child" is a well-known idiom that slightly adapts a line from the Old Testament book of Proverbs: "Whoever spares the rod hates his son, but he who loves him is diligent to discipline him." (A rod was a bundle of twigs or a stick, used to deliver a beating.) This is but one of many Bible verses that can—just like texts from the Quran and other sacred texts—serve to defend what may otherwise seem indefensible. A website promoting the Christian Domestic Discipline movement, for example, advises men on how to beat their wives. By way of justification, the site quotes Biblical expressions like "Blows and wounds cleanse away evil" and "A whip for the horse, a bridle for the ass, and a rod for the fool's back."

We like to think of childhood as a time of innocence, free from adult cares. The phrase "child's play" means something that's easy to do—almost as easy, indeed, as taking candy from a baby. Yet in past centuries, and in certain parts of the world today, children had no choice but to work; they suffered from virulent diseases; many of them died. Even the healthy ones had to be whipped into shape. That's the gist of the proverb "Spare the rod and spoil the child." Through much of history, corporal punishment—even of young children—was taken for granted. Boys and girls were expected to know their place, and that place was subservient to adults.

Sometimes language shines a clear light into the beliefs of the past. I always thought the Victorian era was responsible for the saying "Children should be seen and not heard." But I was wrong. It goes back—way back—to ancient Greece. A character in *The Clouds*, a comic play by Aristophanes, says, "I'm going to talk about traditional schooling, how things used to be in my prime, when there was talk of 'right' and virtue was the norm. First, children were seen and not heard." (The play was written more than two thousand years ago, and even then people were complaining about the liberal mores of their time.) Moving forward through the ages, the maxim was most often applied to girls—in the Middle Ages and the Renaissance, boys were not required to shut up and stay visible. Only in the nineteenth century did the saying become broadly applied to children of both sexes.

"A burnt child dreads the fire" is another ancient proverb, graphically expressing the idea that when you've endured a serious injury or problem, you'll be careful to avoid it in the future. You might think that the phrase "treat with kid gloves"—to handle something with delicacy and care—also displays an awareness that children can readily get hurt. No such luck. The kids in the idiom are actually young goats, and "kid gloves" are made from their skins: no other type of leather is so soft.

The search for a fountain of youth, a spring whose healing waters would overturn the ravages of age, inspired adventurers for centuries. Today it's the metaphorical stuff of website promises and newspaper headlines, as in a story the *New York Times* ran in March 2017: "Ping-Pong as the Fountain of Youth." The "bloom of youth" likens young people to a brief flowering season that can fade all too quickly. By contrast, "the bloom is off the rose" suggests fatigue and disillusionment. When you say "Youth must be served," you're allowing young people to have their own way without advice or interference from their elders. Youth has indeed been served when a person "comes of age," a more elegant, thoughtful manner of saying "grows up."

Household Names

If you're living "the life of Riley," you're enjoying life to the hilt. The phrase (spelled Reilly on occasion) first appeared in print in 1911, thanks to a reporter for a Connecticut newspaper who was assigned to cover a missing cow: "After 'living the life of Riley' for over a year, successfully evading the pitchforks and the bullets of the farmers . . . the cow today fell victim to a masterfully arranged trap." Those were the days, in agriculture and journalism alike. But who was Riley?

The answer involves Irish Americans in the late nineteenth century. Huge numbers of Irish people had reached the United States a generation or two earlier, refugees from famine and discrimination at home. A popular vaudeville singer of the day was an immigrant named Pat Rooney, and Irish American audiences lined up to hear him belt out a comic song entitled "Is That Mr. Reilly?" Its chorus contained the lines "Well, if that's Mr. Reilly, / they speak of so highly." Maybe there was a particular Reilly whose good fortune inspired the song, but if so, he's long forgotten. More likely, the songwriter chose an Irish name that conveniently rhymed with "highly." The phrase "life of Riley" took off from there.

What is "the prime of life"? In Muriel Spark's classic novel *The Prime of Miss Jean Brodie*, an Edinburgh teacher (memorably played by Maggie Smith in the film version) tells her adoring pupils, "These years are still the years of my prime." She's at her best, in other words: her most energetic, her most alluring, her most powerful. The idiom used to refer to young adulthood, but now it often stretches into middle age. Later, having suffered disgrace, Miss Brodie admits that she is past her prime. To be past your prime is to have reached an age where your daily life, far from being the usual uphill struggle, threatens to go downhill fast.

In language, as in Hollywood movies, youth receives a lot more attention than middle age. Youth implies promise; adulthood holds the shadows of mortality. Those shadows deepen in old age. English is full of idioms for the last years of life, most of them unflattering. To say that someone has entered "second childhood" is to conjure up a picture of sorry dependence: an elderly person who can no longer look after his or her own needs. Once people begin to approach their second childhood, they're "over the hill"; their days are numbered. A "senior moment" is a recently coined phrase that evokes sudden, brief forgetfulness. After the seventy-nine-year-old actor Warren Beatty was wrongly accused of being responsible for the Best Picture fiasco at the 2017 Academy Awards, a journalist for the *Hollywood Reporter* wrote, "Admit it, all you ageists, many of you assumed he was having a senior moment."

Then there's the word *old*, which features in an extraordinary variety of idioms. Some of them are sweet and affectionate. An "old flame" is somebody you once held a torch for. A woman who has "an old head on young shoulders" is wise beyond her years, and the value of experience is equally clear if you describe a man as "an old hand" at something. People like to remember— or, at least, imagine—the "good old days." In the good old days, it's easy to believe, we had a "rare old time." We may have been listening to some "golden oldies," a phrase born on American radio in the mid-1960s. A Philadelphia DJ named Jimmy Blavat is generally credited with inventing the term; idioms sometimes come from unlikely sources.

But it's hard to overlook all the other expressions about the elderly, the ones that evoke the scars of time and the inevitable setbacks of aging. "You can't teach an old dog new tricks" evokes the difficulty of learning when a person is no longer young. It's as futile as trying to put new wine in old bottles. The "old boy network" (or "old boys' club") is not made up of boys, nor is it ever mentioned with approval. "Tough as an old boot" can suggest grudging praise if the subject at hand is a person, but not if the phrase is applied to a steak or some other foodstuff.

If you "open old wounds," you're insisting that injuries or grievances that happened in the past must not be forgotten. A similar idiom, stemming from the Industrial Revolution, warned people not to "rake over old coals." A newer North American phrase, "same old same old," implies tedium, boredom, annoyance. You don't expect those reactions when you listen to an old wives' tale, but you don't expect the truth, either. All these expressions, and many more, display a bruised awareness of the cost of experience. In short, the English language suggests, there's no fool like an old fool. If you don't believe me, you might think these paragraphs are the oldest trick in the book.

Spoonfuls of sugar

Some types of cheese taste better when they've been aged. Their flavor is more pronounced and more robust. In the United States and Britain, people talk about "aged cheese," "sharp cheese" and "strong cheese" to identify a cheddar that has been stored for a year or more before going on the market. But in Canada, cheese makers use the expressions "old cheese" and "extra old cheese." In Quebec, old cheddar is not *vieux* but *fort*, or strong—and when newcomers to Canada see bilingual cheese labels that say "Old Fort," they sometimes assume this is a brand name.

The phrase "as old as Methuselah" takes the name of a mythical patriarch (mythical except among the most literal-minded

Bible readers, that is). In the Book of Genesis, Methuselah, the grandfather of Noah, survives until the ripe old age of 969. To call someone "as old as Methuselah" means the same as calling that person "old as the hills." Indeed, it's hard to find much difference between Methuselah and another mythical, white-bearded figure: old Father Time.

"Elvis has left the building," on the other hand, is a phrase that involves the name of an actual person: the singer Elvis Presley. The idiom means that, hey folks, it's time to go home—there's no point hanging around the stage hoping for another encore. Sportscasters use the line to say that a game is effectively over—not much time is left on the clock, and the latest goal, home run or touchdown has sealed the result. Abandon hope, all ye who expect more hit songs to emerge from the lips that uttered "Hound Dog" and "Jailhouse Rock": Elvis has left the building.

The oldest lyrics for a number one song were written not by Chuck Berry or Buddy Holly (Elvis almost never wrote his own songs), but by an anonymous translator in England in the early seventeenth century, working on a text composed in the Middle East well over two thousand years ago. The folksinger Pete Seeger put those lyrics to music in the 1950s, and the Byrds later made the song a hit. It had the title "Turn! Turn! Turn!" The words come from the Book of Ecclesiastes, and the song is about time:

To every thing there is a season, and a time to every purpose under the heaven:

A time to be born, and a time to die . . .
A time to rend, and a time to sew; a time to keep silence, and a
  time to speak;
A time to love, and a time to hate; a time of war, and a time of
  peace.

Ecclesiastes is a text of radical doubt; it offers few of the standard religious comforts. The phrase "under the sun" occurs in it thirty times over, the sun's movement being an ancient way to assess the passing of time.

"To every thing there is a season" became a famous proverb, used in a multitude of contexts. The Canadian author Alistair MacLeod, for instance, made it the title of a Christmas story set on his beloved Cape Breton Island. Another proverb can be traced to a later chapter of Ecclesiastes: "Then I commended mirth, because a man hath no better thing under the sun than to eat, and to drink, and to be merry." Combined with a verse from the prophet Isaiah—"Let us eat and drink; for tomorrow we shall die"—the result is a saying that resonates through time: "Eat, drink and be merry: for tomorrow we die."

Idioms offer a consistent lesson in realism. Ever since the seventeenth century, English speakers have learned that "If the mountain won't come to Muhammad, Muhammad must go to the mountain." The idea comes not from the Quran itself but from one of the many stories told about the founder of Islam after his death. Challenged to perform a miracle, he gracefully accepted the inevitable instead.

• • •

Sometimes the past aches in our bones. We wake up in the middle of the night, regretting something we did or said, or failed to say and do. If only we could turn back the hands of time! But clocks do not tick backward, and as the image of a nondigital clock suggests, we can never recapture what has gone. "The ship has sailed." We can't stand around staring at the sea: it's time to move on. Now and then we may hear a long-forgotten song, or catch an old movie, or even just repeat a word that strikes us as a "blast from the past"—nostalgia, like regret, has the power to take us by storm. But the experience can't last. Soon it's "over and done with" and fated to become "a thing of the past."

Merchant of Words

How many periods of age are there in a lifetime? You can make a case for three or four or five or more. William Shakespeare settled on seven.

All the world's a stage,
And all the men and women merely players;
They have their exits and their entrances,
And one man in his time plays many parts,
His acts being seven ages.

These lines begin a long speech by Jaques, a melancholy lord in Shakespeare's bittersweet comedy *As You Like It*. Jaques identifies the ages as those of an infant, a child, a young lover, a soldier, a middle-aged judge, an aging miser, and finally: "second childishness and mere oblivion, / Sans teeth, sans eyes, sans taste, sans everything."

"Second childishness and mere oblivion" is a bleak vision of old age. But Shakespeare also came up with a magnificent image summarizing the power of a strong, beautiful woman to resist the onslaught of time and forestall the triumph of oblivion. In his play *Antony and Cleopatra*, one of Antony's friends praises the Egyptian queen by saying "Age cannot wither her, nor custom stale / Her infinite variety." The words have been applied not just to Cleopatra but to countless women since. In 2017, when Serena Williams defeated a string of younger players and won the Australian Open tennis championship at the age of thirty-five, one of India's national newspapers published an admiring tribute below the headline "Age Cannot Wither Serena."

As long as we still have our wits, we can, at least, remember. The actions of recalling and forgetting provide another rich source of idioms. To "bear something in mind" conveys a sense of physical weight—we hold our thoughts and memories in our heads the way we carry a suitcase in our hands. But sometimes time hangs heavy on our hearts and minds. Expressions like "the weight of time," "the body of knowledge" and "the burden of understanding" show how ideas are embodied in language. Idioms carry a freight of meaning just as our bodies haul the years.

Physical activity is also central to "a walk down memory lane."

(Or a stroll, or a trip.) When something reminds us of a person or an experience we'd forgotten, we say it "jogs the memory." "Jog," in that context, has nothing to do with a gentle run—a much older meaning of the word is to shake or jerk.

And suppose your memory stubbornly refuses to be jogged? In that case, we might say you've lost your train of thought. The word *train* refers to a sequence or a succession, and the phrase dates back to the seventeenth century, long before the invention of railways. The notion that memories are like skittish creatures always looking to run away lies behind the phrases "slipped my mind" and "in one ear, out the other." Even more dramatic is the rueful expression "I have a brain like a sieve." We say "an elephant never forgets," I suspect, not just in tribute to the supposed vast bulk of an elephant's memory but also because, like it or not, it's only human to forget. From time to time, it happens. It's natural . . . What was I saying again?

Household Names

Dozens of English idioms make use of people's names, but often we have no idea who those people were. They may be historical, mythical, or entirely invented. For centuries, the most popular name for boys was John, and the language is full of idioms about John, Johnny or Jack (the nickname of many boys whose formal name is John). Phrases that use some variant of the name are generic; they can seldom be traced back to any individual. A "Johnny-come-lately" is a newcomer, whereas a "Johnny on the spot" might be anyone in the right place at the right time. A "Jack of all trades" can turn his hand to anything—but when the phrase is followed by "master of none," the speaker is implying that Jack should have specialized at something. "All work and no play makes Jack a dull boy" appeared in a collection of proverbs published in 1659, many generations before Jack Nicholson obsessively typed out the sentence in the horror movie *The Shining*.

Then there's "before you can say Jack Robinson": at once, right away, now. Scholars have lavished long hours on trying to identify a real-life figure behind this idiom, which dates from eighteenth-century England. But nobody is sure of the answer, just as nobody can be certain who Jack the Ripper was—or "the real McCoy," either.

"There's no time like the present," people often remark. But although the idiom may be literally true, and the idea behind it is of keen interest to philosophers, it's generally used not as a declaration about time but as a request to start moving, stop delaying and get to work. The present fares poorly in English idioms compared to both the past and the future. We like to remember; we like to imagine; and sometimes both memory and imagination serve as useful escapes from whatever's in front of our noses.

If something is not in plain view—if it hasn't happened yet— we might say it's "just around the corner." Keep watching: it will happen "any minute now." Or, if we're looking forward to the future with eager impatience, we're "counting down the days."

If there's something you need to do immediately, you might say "I'll get right on it." Whereas if the task is likely to prove tedious or unpleasant, your promise would take a vaguer form: "I'll get around to it." Whatever may be coming down the road, or the pipeline, the surest thing we can say about the future is also the most banal: "Time will tell."

Proverbs encapsulate the wisdom of ages, or at least the stuff we keep saying to each other. We don't need to be told to repeat bad habits. So while proverbs commonly inform us about how we *should* be behaving, they also reveal what we actually do, or fail to do.

It's hard to think of any idiom suggesting we should get up late, for that kind of advice is seldom needed. "Rise and shine," by contrast, has endured for the better part of two centuries. "The early bird gets the worm" is even older. In a literal sense, it depends on the knowledge that worms slither up through the soil to ground level on wet nights; robins and other birds are more likely to eat their fill if they begin to search for food before dawn. Metaphorically speaking, the phrase can be seen as advice not to be late for anything. The persistence of the idiom has led to the recent birth of "early bird discounts" and "early bird specials," all encouraging us to spend our money before we need to.

Regional expressions are often the liveliest of all—sadly, many of them are now dying out. Among English speakers in the Gaspé region of eastern Quebec, an early riser was said to be "up at crow piss." In the English county of Cornwall, such a person was "up before dressed." And to many African Americans in Georgia and South Carolina, dawn is known as "day clean."

Merchant of Words

The expression "as merry as the day is long" comes from Shakespeare's history play *King John*, now a fairly obscure work, but very popular in the past—though I assume he meant to evoke a day in June or July, not one in January.

At the far side of the turning year, beyond what Shakespeare called "the teeming autumn, big with rich increase," lies "the winter of our discontent." This expression has enjoyed an afterlife far beyond its original context: a bitter monologue by a cunning schemer who will soon grab the throne of England and adopt the name Richard III. Memorable phrases usually spawn imitators, and this one is no exception. A 2010 book about a family living offline had the title *The Winter of Our Disconnect*, and a political comedy show put on in 2016 by Second City in Chicago was called *The Winner . . . of Our Discontent*. But my favorite adaptation of the phrase occurred when an English camping store put a big sign in its front window: "Now is the winter of our discount tents."

"Morning, noon and night" is an old expression in standard English, meaning "all the time." Several other idioms involving morning have recently expanded to cover different parts of the day. For example, you can suffer from a hangover not just on "the morning after" but in the afternoon, too, and the "morning-after pill" is effective at preventing an undesired pregnancy for at least three days after unprotected sex. "Morning sickness" refers to the nausea many women experience early in pregnancy, especially, but not exclusively, in the first hours of the day. As for a "Monday morning quarterback," that phrase originated in the United States to mean fans who liked to criticize a football team's performance or a coach's decisions the day after a game—but it can now evoke anyone who claims expertise in hindsight. Every day of the week, the comment boxes on news websites are overrun by Monday morning quarterbacks.

Another American expression that has moved far beyond its original context is "high noon." Once it was nothing more or less than the midpoint of the day, a moment when the sun stood high in the sky. Occasionally it still has that meaning. In 2012, a writer in the *New York Review of Books* spoke of "the magical blue of a Mediterranean sky at high noon." But the rampant success of the Gary Cooper Western *High Noon* gave the phrase a different tone. It now refers to a critical event, potentially violent, often a showdown between two forces or individuals. A book about policy issues in cyberspace has the name *High Noon on the Electronic Frontier*; a history of the Cuban missile crisis is entitled *High Noon in the Cold War*.

Whether in songs or novels, political speeches or economic forecasts, dawn is a symbol of beginning. "The dawn of a new era" is one of those phrases that has been spouted so often, it has become a cliché. But whereas morning suggests the early stages of something, and noon its height, evening is often seen as symbolic of age and decline. "Sunset years" are a person's last.

In "the twilight zone," it's unclear where one realm ends and another one begins. "The twilight of the gods" started off in Norse mythology—sometime in the future, so the story goes, the world will be afflicted by invasions, floods, a cataclysmic battle, volcanic eruptions, cosmic upheavals, and the death of numerous gods. You might call it the original disaster porn. "Twilight of the gods" went on to become, among other things, the title of an opera by Richard Wagner, an album by a Swedish metal band, a Doctor Who novel, a video game and a book about the Beatles.

Spoonfuls of sugar

A full-blown nuclear war would, in all likelihood, lead to a time when smoke and dust in the atmosphere blocked the sun's rays from reaching Earth. That period—dark, bitterly cold, inhospitable to the growth of plants or the life of animals—goes by the name "nuclear winter." It would be a season that blackened our planet for years.

As with the times of day, so do the seasons of the year evoke different facets of our lives. "Spring fever" evokes an urge to act, a feeling of decisiveness and energy often associated with youth. "No spring chicken" is one of the many oblique phrases we can use to evoke advancing age. So is the expression "autumn years." Winter—in its lack of growth, its icy chill—brings to mind the end of life. The coldest time of year is the "dead of winter" (now a popular "metacooperative strategy board game" set in a post-apocalyptic world inhabited by zombies). Nobody ever talks about the dead of summer.

All this goes to show that time is one of the main preoccupations of language. Seeking to explore and understand it, people have invented a host of idioms that embody the sense of life emerging, growing, changing, fading, coming to an end. Indeed, English contains dozens of expressions that speak about time itself.

Think of "killing time." It may well have been adapted from the earlier "pass time," a verb phrase that led to our familiar noun "pastime": a painless, agreeable way to let time slide away. Killing time has become synonymous with boredom, though often, strangely enough, without the moral judgment implied in the phrase "wasting time." Behind the concepts of both killing and wasting time stands the idea that our time on Earth is limited, and it's wrong not to spend it properly. The great American writer Henry David Thoreau, who was no believer in orthodox religion, doubted "if you could kill time without injuring eternity."

When you "make time" for something or someone, you're not manufacturing a commodity called time—you're merely creating the chance for a meeting, an action, an opportunity. But the phrasal verbs of English can be fiendishly intricate. People learning English as a foreign tongue often find its complex verbs the most difficult aspect of the language to master, far worse than inconsistent spellings and bulging dictionaries. "Making good time" refers to the distance traveled on a journey, and "making up time" involves reducing lateness. As for "making time with," that's a piece of American slang for flirtation or sexual advances. It's all too easy to get these phrases mixed up.

Another short phrase with unusual complexity is "big time." In contemporary English, it can be used as a phrase on its own. "I messed up big-time," you might say if your mistake has a lamentable impact. A "big-time problem," accordingly, is a major one. Before this recent shift in meaning, though, "big time" had much happier connotations. "Since hitting the big time in 1979," wrote a music journalist for *XXL* magazine, "hip-hop has matured over the years in many ways." The phrase uses the word *time* without really being *about* time, except in its implicit recognition that our lives are always, inevitably, enmeshed in time.

"Time is money," people sometimes say, or "There's no time to lose," or "We don't have all the time in the world." Those are sayings aimed at spurring action. English has various idioms in which time is invoked as a sour reminder if not an actual threat. "I have no time for this": I want no part of it. "It's not worth my time"—or even, somewhat illogically, "It's not worth the time of day." In many spheres of life, you don't want to be behind the times. Nor do you want to be so desperate that you're forced to bargain for time. But anyone who's "serving time" or "doing time"—anyone in prison, that is—is unlikely to feel that time flies.

By contrast, "all in good time" suggests a desire to wait, not rush, and see how things unfold. "Time heals all wounds" is an even more consoling phrase, reminding us that suffering eventually does come to an end. And one of the most common of all idioms—so common, in fact, that we hardly notice it's an idiom at all—is the phrase "a good time." It's how we remember pleasure, what we want for ourselves, and what we ask for those we love.

That was going to be the last time I mentioned time in this chapter. But I thought of one more expression in the nick of time.

Stealing Your Heart

Nothing stirs our emotions more than love. Nothing thrills our bodies more than sex. And so nothing can be more difficult to talk about and write about—even for professional authors—than physical intimacy. Ever since 1993 London's *Literary Review* has sponsored an annual Bad Sex in Fiction Award, highlighting the worst descriptions of sex in the previous year's books. The unlucky nominees have included many well-known writers, notably Tom Wolfe ("The flood in her loins washed morals, despair, and all other abstract assessments away in a cloud of some sort of divine cologne of his") and Manil Suri ("Only Karun's body, locked with mine, remains. We streak like superheroes past suns and solar systems, we dive through shoals of quarks and atomic nuclei. In celebration of

our breakthrough fourth star, statisticians the world over rejoice"). The experience of sex and the language describing it are often at serious odds.

If we're not talking about sex in explicit or clinical terms, we may need to look for euphemisms. More of that later. But first, let's think about feelings.

It's one thing to "have a crush" on someone. That expression suggests a teenage infatuation, pleasant enough while it lasts, but nothing too serious. If the crush is reciprocated, it can turn into "puppy love" or "calf love." There's an implied condescension in equating novice lovers with juvenile animals. But there's no condescension in our idioms for the real thing, the hurting amazement that goes with "falling in love." The physicality of that common phrase—we hear it so often, we seldom stop to think about it—suggests the joyous, agonizing, scary loss of balance that love provokes. It sweeps you off your feet. Your world turns upside down. You're head over heels in love.

Head, heels, feet: idioms for passionate emotion often involve parts of the human body—and, no, I don't mean sex organs. When you kiss a girl, you "lock lips" with her. When you're keen on a guy, you "make eyes at" him. It might be love at first sight, even on a blind date. If all goes well, you "hit it off together." (One of the main reasons English is so hard to master as a foreign language is that its speakers need to grasp the difference between similar-sounding phrases like "hit it off" and "hit on," "break up" and "break down.") Soon you have the hots for each

other—you may even burn with desire. These are not the flames of hell; these are the fires of love.

And then there's the heart.

New York was in the doldrums in the 1970s. The crime rate was high, the streets were crumbling, the economy was fragile. That's when the city launched an advertising campaign based on a slogan—well, really a logo—that was so brilliant, it helped turn New York's fortunes around. The slogan, of course, was I♥NY. In those long-ago, pre-internet days, there were no such things as emojis. But the heart image served the same function that emojis do in text messages today: it conjured up an emotion without resorting to words. The heart is an ancient symbol of love, and everyone displaying the slogan was showing their fondness for a great and troubled city. Heart symbols soon proliferated in logos for a variety of cities, causes, regions, foods, companies, countries and people.

In English idioms, the heart doesn't always refer to love—it plays a vibrant role in a host of other sayings. But expressions for love that rely on the heart are among the most intimate and necessary ones of all. If you fall deeply in love with somebody, she "wins your heart." If a person falls just as deeply in love with you, you've "stolen his heart." A more old-fashioned expression still heard from time to time is "an affair of the heart"—often with the implication of an illicit romance. The advance publicity for an episode of *Dr. Phil* once posed the question "At what point does a friendly relationship become an affair of the heart or emotional infidelity?"

Household Names

A "peeping Tom" is a voyeur, someone who takes sexual pleasure in furtively watching others. The expression comes from a story that is almost certainly untrue. It's said that nearly a thousand years ago, Godiva—a powerful and beautiful lady in the English city of Coventry—was upset by the heavy taxes that Leofric, her lordly husband, had imposed on the townspeople. Tired of her appeals, Leofric retorted that he would cut the taxes only if Godiva rode naked on horseback through the city. To her husband's astonishment, she did exactly that—having asked the local citizens not to watch her as she passed by. The only person who broke faith was a tailor named Thomas: the original peeping Tom. Leofric kept his part of the bargain but, depending on the version of the story you hear, Thomas the tailor was either blinded or killed.

Lady Godiva did indeed exist, and she's recorded as doing an assortment of good works, but the notion of a peeping Tom arose only in the eighteenth century, seven hundred years after Godiva's death. The story needed a victim, a villain, or both. The newly created idiom evoked a condition, or affliction, for which there was as yet no name—the French word *voyeur* arrived in English later than "peeping Tom."

When the affair is going wrong, you suffer from an aching heart. And if it comes to a bitter end, you might be left heartbroken. Having a "broken heart" is another of those commonplace idioms that are intertwined in the whole fabric of English—it's hard to imagine the language without it. How many blues and country songs, how many movies and TV shows depend on the notion of heartbreak? It's a striking expression, one that conveys the overwhelming force of grief and suffering. Easy to carry on living despite the inconvenience of a fractured wrist or ankle. The pain of a broken heart is far worse.

Expressions for sex appeal often convey a sense of danger. Admittedly, that's not obvious in "eye candy" or "sex kitten," although even kittens have claws. But think about "jailbait," "vamp" (short for vampire), or "blonde bombshell." That last idiom has been applied to a number of Hollywood actresses over the years. It was coined to promote Jean Harlow, the star of the 1933 movie *Bombshell*. Its ad campaign announced the arrival of "Lovely, luscious, exotic Jean Harlow as the Blonde Bombshell of filmdom." What gives the idiom its power is the sense that sooner or later, bombshells explode—Harlow, Jayne Mansfield, Brittany Murphy and Marilyn Monroe all died before their fortieth birthday.

Donkey's Hind Leg

Expressions for beauty come and go over time. Back in seventeenth-century England, a good-looking man or woman was known as "snout-fair." I don't recommend trying out that idiom on someone you're hoping to date. Oddly enough, the original meaning of "snout" was an elephant's trunk, even though the word arrived in English centuries before the first elephant.

It was the midwestern United States that gave birth to the nineteenth-century idiom "hotter than Dutch love in harvest." But this didn't refer to passion. It referred to excessive summer heat. Perhaps Dutch lovers are more ardent than Belgians, perhaps they sweat more than Germans—or, more likely, the phrase took off from the use of "Dutch oven" to mean a big cooking vessel.

You don't have to be blond to be "drop-dead gorgeous." This is a more recent expression, invented in 1985 by a journalist for *Time* who wanted to underscore the beauty of the actress Michelle Pfeiffer. "Drop dead!" began life as an insult and, a couple of generations ago, somehow became an intensifying phrase— a more startling way to say "very." You can, if you want, now talk about a food being "drop-dead delicious" or a person being "drop-dead honest." But the most common use of the phrase is still the one that ties it to gorgeousness, implying that beauty is perilous and not to be trusted. After all, as a much older idiom puts it, "Beauty is only skin-deep."

That expression goes back to one of Shakespeare's contemporaries, an English courtier named Sir Thomas Overbury. In 1613, in his long poem *A Wife*, Overbury wrote: "All the carnall beauty of my wife / Is but skin deep." Overbury was imagining things: he never married. Soon after completing the poem, he died while a prisoner in the Tower of London, perhaps as a result of poisoning.

History suggests that Overbury was less attracted to blonde bombshells than to what some have called "babe magnets"—sexually attractive men, that is. Such men have gone by many names over the years, including "dreamboats" or "heartbreakers." For a time, one of the more popular words for a ruggedly good-looking man was "hunk," a term that would have baffled earlier generations. The modern meaning arose only in the 1960s. Prior to then, a hunk could refer to a miser, a large chunk of bread, an immigrant to North America from central or eastern Europe, or (in Scotland) a lazy woman.

Looking for Mr. Goodbar, the title of a novel by Judith Rossner and a lurid movie starring Diane Keaton, riffs on the idiom "looking for Mr. Right." This sounds like a modern American expression. But it can be traced back to Britain in the late eighteenth century, when an obscure poet named John Crane introduced the phrase "Mr. Right" in his "Address to the Bachelors." What *is* contemporary and American is a playful variant on the idea: "I'm looking for Mr. Right, not Mr. Right Now"—a helpful line if you ever need to turn away an unwanted male.

Sometimes, though, men refuse to turn away. In many countries, a girl who is raped brings shame to her family. She can be persecuted, punished, shunned, even killed for the "crime" of being the victim of male lust. That's the origin of the idiom "a fate worse than death." Today, the line is used in jest to refer to any bad experience. But a century ago, it meant rape. In his novel *Tarzan of the Apes*, the fountainhead of so many third-rate movies, Edgar Rice Burroughs describes how an ape "threw her roughly across his broad, hairy shoulders, and leaped back into the trees, bearing Jane Porter away toward a fate a thousand times worse than death."

Sure, it sounds funny now. But for girls across much of the world, "a fate worse than death" still sums up the meaning of rape.

When a couple are officially "an item"—when they're so perfect together they seem "made for each other"—we can say their relationship is "a match made in heaven." In the coolly secular light of the twenty-first century, we're more likely to speak of temporary unions as "friends with benefits" or a partnership of "significant others," both prosaic ways to describe a sexual relationship. More playfully, if a happy couple spends their time "whispering sweet nothings" to each other, they can be described as "lovebirds." Lovebirds—the kind with beaks and feathers, I mean—spend long periods of time in each other's company, call loudly, and mate repeatedly. But they can also be aggressive. Sometimes, when they don't want to mate, they fight. As an old proverb puts it, "All's fair in love and war."

Things can go wrong with any couple. Small wonder, then, that English is full of idioms describing the challenges we all face in keeping love alive. If two people are constantly "at each other's throats," their relationship is "on the rocks," an idiom derived from sailing—metaphorically speaking, the ship holding the couple has been swept ashore and is at high risk of being destroyed. (The much smoother "scotch on the rocks," by contrast, refers merely to ice cubes.)

At that point in a couple's relationship, there's "no love lost between them." This is a curious expression because from the time it arose, around 1600, until the mid-nineteenth century, it could mean either of two completely opposite things. In his comic play *She Stoops to Conquer*, the Anglo-Irish author Oliver Goldsmith gave a wonderful stage direction at the end of a brief exchange between a young couple named Tony and Constance: "They retire, and seem to fondle." Then Tony's mother appears and asks what's going on. Tony replies, "We grumble a little now and then, to be sure. But there's no love lost between us." In other words, their love is steadfast and mutual—or so he claims.

That sense of "no love lost" has since evaporated, leaving the contrary meaning in sole possession of the field. In May 2017, for example, a celebrity website reported on a feud between singers Taylor Swift and Calvin Harris by saying, "There's certainly no love lost between the one-time lovebirds." In that sentence the word *lost* is irrelevant, potentially even misleading, for the idiom now denotes a complete absence of love. Swift and Harris appear to be living out the truth of a proverb widely attributed to the ancient Greek philosopher Socrates: "The hottest love has the coldest end."

Combing the Giraffe

The Moulin Rouge. The Left Bank. Édith Piaf. Brigitte Bardot.

Paris has long exerted a romantic allure on the imaginations of English speakers, and to some people, the language of the city still conveys an erotic mystique. Historically, French morals were often felt to be looser than those of Britain or America, and during the nineteenth century, an intimate three-way arrangement became known in English as a *ménage à trois*. In the same era, a novel by Alexandre Dumas introduced the expression "*cherchez la femme*" into French, and it quickly became an English catchphrase suggesting that if a man could only find the woman who was to blame for a problem, everything would be resolved.

A word or phrase with two meanings, one of them suggestive of sex, is a *double entendre*. But the allure of French remains even when the actual words are distorted. Nobody from France (or Quebec) ever says "ooh la la" to show surprise or pleasure, but in the ears of English speakers, the phrase sounds vaguely French and has *risqué* overtones. As for "My Cherie Amour," it was an early hit by the Detroit musician Stevie Wonder. It's doubtful if Motown boys ever expressed their undying affection for a girl by using the French words for "darling love," but those words do lend the song a certain *je ne sais quoi*.

Sooner or later, one of the partners in a stone-cold relationship is likely to cheat on the other. "Cheating on" may well be followed by "walking out on." (Again, this expression reveals the importance of getting prepositions right—"walk out with" is an old British idiom to describe a dating couple.) At that point, it's the lonely bed, the empty bottle, the aching heart. Or, as the title of one of my all-time favorite country songs says, "I've Got Tears in My Ears from Lyin' on My Back in My Bed While I Cry Over You."

Unhappiness can arise for any number of reasons, but money is high on the list. The saying "When poverty comes in at the door, love flies out of the window" catches the idea perfectly. It's hard to be head over heels in love if you're also head over heels in debt. In 2006, a journalist for the *Times* of London used an old British idiom in evoking "a choice between a triumphant return to high finance and love in a cottage." The expression "love in a cottage" neatly sums up the difficulty of trying to sustain a relationship when money is hard to come by.

Not all relationships end on the rocks, thank goodness. Sometimes it's possible to "kiss and make up." Even if one of the partners has been "a love rat"—has been conducting an affair on the side, that is—two people can manage to "patch things up," as though a relationship were a suit of clothing. Life may have burned holes in the suit, but the holes can still be mended.

So the rocks have been averted, the clothes patched up, and the love that was lost has been found again. It's time to "tie the knot"—to get married, that is. In the formal language of the past, a young man would ask for a woman's hand in marriage. More casually, a man would "pop the question" and a woman would agree to "get hitched." Hitching, in that sense, does not mean sticking out your thumb and hoping for a ride; it's the procedure to be followed when putting a horse into its harness. Sometimes marriage is described as "the tie that binds." Goodbye, freedom—idioms about marriage, it seems, have a notable physicality.

One small sign of our generally relaxed view of premarital sex is that the idiom "shotgun wedding" is rarely heard today. The phrase originated in the United States and referred to a marriage performed in haste, as the bride was already pregnant. The shotgun in question would be held, figuratively speaking, by the bride's father, and pointed at the groom. The British equivalent was a "knobstick wedding," a knobstick being a round-headed staff or club carried by the wardens of a church. In past centuries, the church, not the government, was responsible for local welfare, and the church liked a father to pay for his offspring. The Chinese idiom for this type of wedding is wryly humorous in tone: "married by order of child."

Even in the absence of shotguns and knobsticks, a man might occasionally decide to back out of a marriage at the last minute. An old expression for runaway groom behavior is "leave her at the altar"—the altar that stands at the front of a church where wedding vows are exchanged. Traditionally, a bride entered the church on her father's arm and left it in the company of her husband. Hence the expression "walk down the aisle," an oblique way of saying "get married." Couples would take the fateful stroll only after both partners had vowed "to have and to hold, from this day forward, for better, for worse, for richer, for poorer, in sickness and in health, to love and to cherish, till death us do part."

The wording of that solemn promise reflects the beliefs and behaviors of the past. Many of today's expressions also have their roots in earlier centuries. But expectations for the marriage ceremony in the twenty-first century are changing, and as they do, new idioms emerge. One of them is "destination wedding"—an event that takes place far away from the couple's home, usually in a glamorous location like a beach-fringed tropical island, an alpine resort or a Tuscan hill town. "Stag parties" have long been part of a groom's preparation for marriage, and today "bachelorette parties" are just as popular. A story on the brides.com website in March 2017 appeared under the headline "Bachelorette etiquette your besties will appreciate." (Best friends, that is.) The old term for an unmarried woman was "spinster," but nobody ever talks about spinster parties. Indeed, in Canada today, "stagette" has begun to make "bachelorette" sound old-fashioned. British women, for some reason, remain fond of the phrase "hen party."

Merchant of Words

In the tragedy *Othello*, one of Shakespeare's most evil schemers uses a memorable expression to describe sexual intercourse: Iago calls it "the beast with two backs." You still come across the idiom on occasion. A story on the *Vice* website in November 2016 described how, allegedly, a cable provider in the Boston area broadcast a segment of hard-core porn during a CNN show on Thanksgiving Day, adding that "CNN now denies airing the beast with two backs to people indulging in turkey."

"Star-crossed lovers" is another Shakespearean invention, the original pair being Juliet and Romeo. Fate was against them from the start. Shakespeare could have underlined their bleak predicament by saying "The course of true love never did run smooth"—except this line appears in another of his plays, *A Midsummer Night's Dream*. The expression has been used in a myriad of ways. Four centuries after the playwright's death, a British banker heralded the financial power of dating apps by saying, "While it may not always lead to the course of true love, the dating scene is definitely doing its bit to boost the UK economy."

Weddings are performed for many reasons, not just love. If the bride and groom want to keep their wedding secret from family and friends, theirs is a "clandestine marriage." The more common term "arranged marriage" refers to a partnership between young people who had no choice in the matter; the match was made by older members of their families, often requiring the payment of a dowry. A "mail-order bride" is a woman chosen by a man from some kind of catalogue. In the past, when Japanese and Korean men in North America sent for a wife from their homeland, the usual term was "picture bride." Another expression fading into history is "lavender marriage": a partnership concealing the queer sexuality of the bride, the groom or both. This was but one among several types of marriage of convenience. "Green card marriages," in the United States, are another: they entail a wedding between an American citizen and an immigrant or refugee who would otherwise be unable to stay in the country.

Some of these idioms perform well in a broader context. An opinion piece in the *Irish Times*, published in 2017, described "the unholy and unhealthy relationship between the Catholic church and the Irish state" as a "marriage of convenience." When the Japanese carmaker Nissan rescued a financially distressed rival, an automobile website ran a story with the headline "Nissan and Mitsubishi: Shotgun Wedding of the Year?" If you think that sounds unpleasant, just imagine the scene evoked by a headline on the *Daily Beast* website in July 2016: "The awkward arranged marriage of Trump and Pence." The story went on to say that the formal announcement of Mike Pence as Donald Trump's running mate had "all the pomp and circumstance of a man meeting a mail-order spouse."

The common thread in all those examples is doubt or scorn about the relationship in question. At such times, marriage idioms can serve as a useful shorthand, eloquently evoking the felt unease.

Many of the expressions relating to sex are old. Many of them are new. Some of the ones you think sound old are actually quite new. "Bodice ripper," for instance, is an expression in the book industry for sexually explicit romances aimed at a female audience. *Bodice* is a centuries-old word, formerly meaning a girdle or whalebone corset, now usually just a vest or the top part of a woman's dress, and readers of these novels can look forward to the fragile heroine's bodice being ripped away by a hell-raking lion of a man. Does the phrase make you think of windswept English moors in the nineteenth century? Think again. The term was first recorded in the *New York Times* in 1979 to describe the work of Vanessa Royall, who was "enjoying a good reputation and lucrative income as the author of the sort of breathless historical romances . . . that are known in the publishing trade as bodice-rippers." "Vanessa Royall" is almost an idiom in its own right: the author's real name is Michael T. Hinkemeyer.

I imagine that after reading a good bodice ripper, some people take their pleasure into their own hands. Among the countless idioms for masturbation—some of them only for women, some only for men, others applicable to both sexes—a few stand out. The judgmental old expression "self-abuse" can be replaced, if you like, by "self-consolation." In previous generations, men were said to "beat the meat" and "spank the rooster," while women were busy "buttering the corn," "flicking the bean" and "buffin' the muffin." These expressions share a zesty energy and a rhetorical structure. My personal favorite, though, depends on the knowledge that in the nineteenth century, one of the most famous poets in English was Henry Wadsworth Longfellow, the author of *Hiawatha*. He's not read much today. But if a man wants to be witty, literary and suggestive all at once, he simply needs to say that he's been "arguing with Henry Longfellow."

Most of these expressions contain an element of innuendo—of suggestive wordplay, that is. ("If I said that your body is gorgeous, would you hold it against me?") It's not always advisable or even possible to talk about sex in a blunt, straightforward way. Official censorship—or self-censorship—can be a source of creativity, a catalyst for the imagination. Innuendos have their uses, and so, on occasion, do euphemisms. Their bad reputation is well deserved, on the whole—in the Victorian period, some people avoided the word *trousers* by calling the garment "indispensables," "inexplicables," "inexpressibles" or "unmentionables." But sometimes, a euphemism allows a point to be made in a cute or inoffensive manner. A lively euphemism for sex in the twenty-first century is "putting your wand in the chamber of secrets"—assuming you've read the Harry Potter books, that is.

Besides, technical vocabulary is often dull to the point of absurdity. Which is more striking, "vasocongestion accompanied by testicular pain" or "lover's nuts"? Another name for this harrowing affliction: "blue balls."

Spoonfuls of Sugar

Many people associate "the love that dare not speak its name" with the playwright Oscar Wilde, who was charged with gross indecency in 1895. But he did not write the words "I am the love that dare not speak its name." This was, in fact, the ending of "Two Loves," a poem by Wilde's young lover, Lord Alfred Douglas. Under cross-examination, Wilde was challenged to explain the line. He told the judge, "'The love that dare not speak its name' in this century is such a great affection of an elder for a younger man as there was between David and Jonathan, such as Plato made the very basis of his philosophy, and such as you find in the sonnets of Michelangelo and Shakespeare. It is that deep spiritual affection that is as pure as it is perfect . . . The world mocks at it, and sometimes puts one in the pillory for it."

Those powerful words don't tell the whole story. Wilde was flamboyantly gay, and there was plenty of evidence in his work to show where his erotic preferences lay. Homosexual acts were a crime in Britain at the time and would remain illegal until the 1960s. Wilde was convicted and sentenced to two years' hard labor. He died in 1900, a broken man. But his explanation has outlived his lover's poem.

For most of its long history, the word *intercourse* meant commerce, fellowship or communication—often it was used in a spiritual sense. A writer in 1649 extolled "the sweet intercourse and communion betwixt God and his Church." That's why, to this day, a village in the Amish country of Pennsylvania has the name of Intercourse. But early in the nineteenth century, the word began to acquire a sexual connotation, and soon that meaning was the only one in most people's minds. In Pennsylvania today, highway signs leading to Intercourse are stolen with sad regularity.

If you don't want to say "sexual intercourse"—and let's admit it, the phrase has a stolid, mechanical air—English offers you countless possibilities. You could say "get laid," if you don't mind impersonating an egg. "Sleep with" has the advantage of brevity and the disadvantage of meaning something totally different from what it actually says. "Sleep together" is another innocent-sounding option with the same disadvantage. Even more innocuous, at first blush, is the expression "have relations with." A character in Barbara Kingsolver's 1998 novel *The Poisonwood Bible* says, "We have relations any old time we feel like it." By "relations," she does not mean relatives.

Household Names

You don't feel like having sex tonight? Tell your partner "Not tonight, Josephine," and pride yourself on the common belief that you're echoing Napoleon Bonaparte, the emperor of France and conqueror of much of Europe. If he could so casually decline the favors of his empress, the former Joséphine de Beauharnais, you can do the same in your own bed. *Not Tonight, Josephine* was the original title of Marilyn Monroe's most famous movie, *Some Like It Hot*.

But Napoleon never said this. Or if he did, nobody recorded it. In fact, Napoleon's love letters are impassioned and eloquent. Soon after his marriage to Joséphine, he wrote to her: "Before long I hope to crush you in my arms and cover you with a million kisses burning as though beneath the Equator." In reality the idiom "Not tonight, Josephine" dates from 1911, when it was the title of a popular song by one Seymour Furth—a song that had nothing to do with Napoleon. Furth also wrote "No Wedding Bells for Me" and "Nothing Like That in Our Family." Seems like a pattern.

In my high school years, the expression "go all the way" would occasionally be uttered with awe, almost reverence. It was a euphemism, of course, but it had undeniable power at a time when many of us, myself included, would have been happy to go even some of the way. We used the language of baseball to describe our hopes and occasional achievements: to go all the way was to hit a home run, so much more desirable than merely reaching first base (kissing), second base (petting) or even third base (heavy petting or oral sex). I say "we," but in retrospect, I don't suppose girls were nearly as fond of baseball talk as boys.

Parents who opt to tell their children as little as possible about sex are liable to resort to vague discussion of "the birds and the bees." This is one euphemism I find regrettable. One of the sources of the expression was probably Emma Drake, a nineteenth-century author who avoided describing sex by writing instead about "the tiny blue eggs in the robin's nest" and "the bees gathering honey from the flowers."

How else might you avoid describing sex? Take your pick from any of the following.

Horizontal refreshment. Carnal knowledge. Doing the nasty. Making a baby. Planting the parsnip. Baking the potato. Pounding the duck. Rolling in the hay. Riding the flagpole. Dipping the wick. Hiding the bishop. Making whoopee. A bit of how's your father (very English, that one). Storming the cotton gin (very American). Having a bit of the old in-and-out. Jelly roll. Happy happy. Jig jig.

These are just some of the older examples. There are dozens, even hundreds, more idioms like that. The supply is inexhaustible, because human beings will always find new ways of talking about the most powerful emotions and sensations—what would our grandparents have thought of "Netflix and chill"? Notice the bouncing rhythms of many of those expressions. They sound joyful. They sound comic. They sound jaunty and defiant. A few of them sound a little bewildering. That seems about right for sex. What they miss, on the whole, is tenderness. But perhaps that grows with age, and I'm sure the majority of those expressions were invented by the young.

In the end, bodies always outstrip language. The full experience of sex is impossible to re-create in words. Writers keep on trying, of course, and they keep on spectacularly failing. Let a final nominee for the Bad Sex in Fiction Award, a novelist named Anthony Capella, prove the point: "She gnawed on Tomasso ravenously, like an animal plundering a carcass, and when she had had enough of that she swung her leg over him, like a rider swinging into a saddle, and galloped."

Poor Tomasso.

Scared of Your Own Shadow

The human body serves as a basis for expressions galore. Our limbs and organs, our sensations and physical features are the material from which English has shaped a kind of body language—one made up not of gestures and postures but of idioms. These turns of phrase rely on our physical selves to evoke ideas and emotions. "Keep body and soul together" is an old way of saying "survive." But it's also an apt means of suggesting how language ties the physical and mental into a vibrant whole.

Take "stiff upper lip." Anyone who shows such a thing is working hard to be resolute and unsentimental, while displaying as little emotion as possible. The idea is often associated with a uniquely British form of stoicism, as in this line from a London newspaper: "Prince Philip found that he could relax from the strains of state business and stiff-upper-lippery." In fact, the phrase began life in the United States in the early nineteenth century, conveying from the start a sense of firmness and emotional restraint, and serving as a fine example of a descriptive idiom that turns a part of the body into a symbol of some attitude or behavior.

"Nose out of joint" performs the same trick. It brings to life a picture of someone who looks extremely annoyed, and it has done so—without any change in meaning—for more than four hundred years. "A sight for sore eyes" is only a little younger, and it too focuses on an organ of the body to express a particular feeling: happiness or relief. These and many other expressions allow words to shape and embody our experience.

I hope you're all ears.

Idioms have a habit of stretching a thought to the point of dramatic absurdity. The meaning of "all ears" is pretty obvious: to listen intently. Likewise, "all mouth and no trousers" is a great British expression for a braggart who can't back up his threats or boasts. Sometimes, oddly enough, people say "all mouth and trousers," which sounds like it should convey the opposite idea, but in fact means exactly the same. The memorable wording of a few expressions for the body can hide ambiguity or confusion.

Think of the line "Butter wouldn't melt in his mouth." It suggests a person with a face of ice. Back in the sixteenth century, the expression did indeed refer to a man or woman who had a cold or haughty manner. Over the centuries, though, the meaning of the idiom split in two. Today some people use it to describe a liar or manipulator whose calm face is at odds with her conduct. But when others employ the phrase, they mean a person who has an innocent appearance, regardless of how he behaves.

Spoonfuls of sugar

Occasionally a writer or speaker will find a deft way to combine two idioms in a memorable line. When you put your foot in your mouth, you make a serious blunder. If you were born with a silver spoon in your mouth, you come from a wealthy family. And in 1988, speaking at her party's national convention, Texas Democrat Ann Richards brought the house down by saying of the Republican presidential nominee George H. W. Bush: "Poor George. He can't help it. He was born with a silver foot in his mouth."

Moving on from the trouserless or butter-filled mouth, we arrive at another idiom that can be a little ambiguous in meaning: "hairy eyeball." This is an American phrase first recorded in 1961, in a newspaper article about the actress Carol Burnett: "She said, 'He gave me the hairy eyeball.' That meant he liked her." (What was this anonymous admirer doing with his eyes or eyebrows?) But in later uses, the meaning was reversed, and today a hairy eyeball generally conveys suspicion or dislike. A 2017 article in the online magazine *New Food Economy* stated, "As crop prices put profits in jeopardy, conventional farmers in the Midwest are giving organics more than the hairy eyeball." In other words, they're giving organic production a long hard look.

The hairy eyeball—even though it's a forceful image—counts as a mild expression of hostility. A more aggressive phrase is "in your face," which arose on the basketball courts of black America in the early 1970s, a few years before the birth of hip-hop. A *Washington Post* article from 1976 spoke of an NBA star "mowing down the 76ers with a burst of 'in-your-face' basketball that could just as well have come from a machine gun." Well, not quite. Soon the idiom lost its associations with hoops and slam dunks and became a common means of expressing any brash, provocative sentiment. Along similar lines, a "barefaced lie" is a brazen one. Your face is what you display to the world. "Put on a brave face," and you're striving to maintain a positive air in spite of grief or disappointment.

Ideas of "saving face" and "losing face" are crucial in the Far East. Both these idioms are direct translations from Chinese. The face, in this context, is a lively, embodied metaphor that sums up a person's—or a nation's—reputation. The two expressions entered English in the nineteenth century and were originally limited to Chinese contexts. But by 1928, in one of his *Forsyte Saga* novels, the English author John Galsworthy could make a character say, "They've got to save face. Saving face is the strongest motive in the world."

Let me give you a heads-up: that's a surprising remark, on the face of it, but it's a shrewd one. When you lose face entirely, "your name is mud."

Tomatoes on Your Eyes

"She cut off her nose to spite her face." Who in the world would choose to mutilate herself so badly? This expression can be taken as a warning not to pursue the kind of destructive actions that backfire against a perpetrator. If you're scheming to cause trouble for another person, you may end up damaging yourself.

Even when you grasp the metaphorical sense of the idiom, the literal meaning sounds improbable. Yet in the Early Middle Ages, actions like this were not unknown. When Viking raiders landed in southern Scotland around the year 870, the mother superior of a local convent urged her nuns to disfigure themselves, thereby making the women unattractive to the sex-starved invaders. She chopped off her nose and upper lip, and many other nuns did the same. This tactic saved their virginity. But not their lives: the furious Vikings burned the convent to the ground. Ebba, the mother superior, was made a saint.

In weaving an intricate skein of connections between body and mind, language goes against the dualist theory that mind and body are distinct, a concept that has been a major influence in the history of Western thought. The seventeenth-century philosopher René Descartes, for example, wrote that "the mind or soul of man is entirely different from the body." Descartes was convinced that the body is a mere machine. He believed that all ideas are disembodied.

Clearly, Descartes paid no attention to how French and all other languages use the body to incarnate feelings and ideas. No matter where we come from and what language we speak, fear ranks among the most powerful of emotions, so it's only natural that fear can be evoked by a host of idioms that express it in physical terms. In English, to be nervous about doing something is "to get cold feet," and a person who's very timid is said to be "scared of his own shadow." Such a person may be continually "on pins and needles." When you're a bundle of nerves, the turmoil inside your body is beautifully expressed by the expression "butterflies in the stomach." You may break out in a cold sweat. Your heart may skip a beat. Or it may seem to lurch upward, in which case you could say "My heart's in my mouth." None of these expressions would make sense if the body and mind were, as the logic of Descartes had it, entirely different from each other.

"Necessity is the mother of invention," an old proverb states. Maybe we should replace necessity by fear, because the list of idioms evoking it is very, very long. To mention a few more, someone or something that alarms you can make your hair stand on end. Even more dramatically, it can make your blood run cold. Truly desperate anxiety may cause you to sweat bullets. You might be "scared out of your skin"—or, because extreme fear can lead to a loss of control over bodily functions, "scared shitless." Now and then, the crudest expressions are also the most accurate.

Donkey's Hind Leg

Language change has weakened a dramatic way of conveying fear: "frighten the living daylights" out of somebody. True, you still hear the idiom from time to time. But it seems mild, even quaint, the sort of thing an elderly aunt might blurt out. That's not how the phrase always sounded. "Daylights" used to be a term for a person's eyes, and so the image had the same kind of force as the modern expression "make her eyes pop out of her head." Over time, "daylights" came to refer to a person's vital organs or life force; then the word vanished from daily use. Eyes or organs: if a fear was powerful enough to expel your daylights, you were terror-struck.

"Keep your chin up!" we might urge in response to all these fear-evoking idioms: don't lose hope. People in Britain sometimes get the same idea across by saying "Keep your pecker up!" The pecker in question can belong to a woman as well as a man. Why? Because it's not a penis but a nose. To quote an 1845 article in the *Times* of London, "Mr. King . . . misstated the fact in saying that he had put a piece of lighted paper to the master's nose while asleep in that house; it was his hot pipe that he applied to the sleeper's nostrils, at the same time crying: Come, old chap, keep your pecker up." Still, the potential for double entendres is enormous. I wonder, for example, what the playwright

W. S. Gilbert really meant when a character in one of his comic operettas, *Trial by Jury*, sang: "Be firm, my moral pecker."

Other expressions involving the face and head are wonderfully graphic. To bury, stick, hide or keep your head in the sand is a criticism, even an insult, going back to ancient Rome—the author and naturalist Pliny the Elder wrongly believed that ostriches would conceal their heads with the aim of escaping hunters. Today the idiom is often applied to climate-change deniers. For example, Jennifer Ronk of the Houston Advanced Research Center was quoted in a Texas newspaper in July 2017 as calling for her state to do more to combat climate change, because "You can't stick your head in the sand." (A month later, Hurricane Harvey proved her point.) Similarly, a New Zealand law student who took her government to court over its failure to meet emissions-reduction targets told Radio New Zealand in 2017, "Entire communities are being left devastated, yet our government is burying its head in the sand, business as usual."

The minuscule chances of losing a lawsuit to a university student meant, in all probability, that the government of New Zealand didn't "turn a hair"—that is, it remained calm. This expression appears to have begun on the racetrack, where some of the best horses show little sign of exertion even after a race. As for "let down your hair"—relax, unwind, chill—that phrase is an offshoot of fashion. In past centuries women were often required to keep their hair pinned up in public, and only when washing it, or in the privacy of a bedroom, could the hair be let down. The process was known as disheveling: the origin of our word *disheveled*, meaning ruffled, unkempt, or in a state of disorder.

To "play it by ear" is to improvise, to act spontaneously according to the needs of the moment. This broad meaning is a departure from the narrower original sense: in the world of music, when you don't have a printed score in front of you, you're said to be playing a piece by ear.

In 1977, the Australian pop singer Helen Reddy released an album entitled *Ear Candy*. The name promptly turned into an idiom, more often associated with eyes than ears. "Ear candy" and "eye candy" are both appealing, yet neither has any real substance. Other familiar expressions involving the eyes are much, much older. "In the twinkling of an eye"—at great speed, that is—comes from the New Testament. "An eye for an eye, a tooth for a tooth" is cited in the Book of Exodus, the New Testament and the Quran, but the idiom goes back even further in time. It forms part of the Code of Hammurabi, compiled by a ruler of Babylon in 1754 BC.

Just as the ears can serve as a symbol for understanding, so too can the tongue serve as a metaphor for speaking, even for language itself. To say anything tongue in cheek is to speak in a playful, nonserious manner. The action contorts the facial muscles, which is why—from both a physical and a metaphorical standpoint—"tongue in cheek" is the opposite of "keep a straight face."

Some idioms preserve an ancient concept of how the body works. "Make a clean breast of it," an eloquent way of saying "confess," is among them. The idiom may seem bizarre at first glance, but if you consult the *Oxford English Dictionary*, you'll find that one of the definitions of "breast," going back well over a thousand years, is "the seat of the affections and emotions; the repository of consciousness, designs, and secrets; the heart; hence, the affections, private thoughts and feelings." That meaning also lurks behind the phrase "keep abreast of" (stay informed). As time went by, the word *chest* took on similar associations, which explains why I can now talk about "getting something off my chest" or "keeping it close to my chest."

At times, "the seat of the affections and emotions" is perceived as lower down in the body. I may hate your guts without disliking your intestines. "Gut feelings"—along with "gut instinct" and "gut reactions"—are powerful things, often leading us into a different course of action from what our brains might have proposed. In American English, guts are a synonym for courage. Hence the expression "no guts, no glory." In British English, the word *gutted*—originally a term for a fish or a building with its middle chopped out—has come to mean bitterly upset or disappointed.

Breasts, chests and guts all fade into the background, though, compared with the heart.

We've seen already how idioms about love resort to the image of a broken heart and a stolen heart. But the heart isn't just a symbol of love and desire. In dozens of English idioms, it denotes emotions of any kind. A heart-to-heart conversation is a dialogue of the most trusting kind. When you see, hear or receive something that does the heart good, it's a particularly welcome gift. You might want to express gratitude "from the bottom of my heart." If it's not gratitude but sympathy you're feeling—for a sick child, perhaps, or a refugee family—you can say "My heart goes out to them." A person "after my own heart" is someone who believes or feels the same way you do. Surely this person's heart is in the right place: she intends to behave well or do the right thing, even if she won't always succeed.

The heart is a complex organ, of course, and not every mention of it is so warm and fuzzy. "Absence makes the heart grow fonder," for instance, expresses a cynical—or just plain realistic—view of relationships. The saying has been around for nearly two centuries. It received a contemporary update in the TV series *Californication*, when one episode was entitled "Absinthe Makes the Heart Grow Fonder." As for the expression "He wears his heart on his sleeve," this, too, may carry an implied criticism: a man like that is bad at hiding his emotions, even if at times he should.

To me the most interesting of all heart-related idioms is also the shortest: "by heart." Why do we say that if you can recite a poem or song from memory, you know it by heart? The idiom has been part of English, its meaning unaltered, since the Middle Ages. It suggests the power of memory—anything that is essential to remember will carry an emotional force and will be known not just "by mind" or "by brain" but also "by heart." Memories are the heartbeat of identity. What we recall is who we are.

• • •

As you might expect, arms and legs are common in idioms that express a sense of action, of movement, of urgency. When you'd give an arm and a leg for something, you desperately want it. If the item in question costs you an arm and a leg, it's tremendously expensive. "In good leg"—or fine leg, or high leg—is to be elated about something. A "shot in the arm" is a badly needed encouragement. Having received one, if you're excited, you might even "kick up your heels."

Tomatoes on Your Eyes

"Break a leg!" we often say before a performance, a speech, an exam or a game. We don't mean it, of course—it's a roundabout way of saying "Good luck!" The expression is not an ancient one—the earliest recorded usage comes from 1921—but the strange thing is, nobody can explain its origin. Some people in Britain have tried to interpret it in light of the cricketing expression "off break"; some Americans have linked it to Abraham Lincoln's assassin, the actor John Wilkes Booth. But these attempts are almost certainly wrong. The least unlikely source is a similar expression in German, *"Hals und Beinbruch!"* (literally, "neck and leg break!"), that air force pilots said to each other in the First World War—a conflict that killed thousands of aircrew on both sides.

Soon after the war's end, the idiom became popular in theaters, at first in the United States. Actors repeat the phrase today in the same contrarian spirit that leads ballet dancers to say *"Merde!"* (the French word for shit) before they go onstage. Literally speaking, both expressions are nonsense. The still unanswered question is why, in the 1920s, Broadway actors began telling each other to break a leg.

What you don't want to do, in any situation, is get off on the wrong foot. It's much better to put your best foot forward. English has a variety of expressions about feet, some of which owe their origin to the endless marching drills that armies have always liked to inflict on their troops. The phrase "foot soldier" carries an implication of both loyalty and drudgery, not always in a military context. In 2016, for example, CBC News reported that "A former Mafia foot soldier is facing deportation 49 years after arriving in Canada." The gentleman may have thought that when he reached Canada, he had "a foot in the door"—an opportunity, that is—but doors have a habit of closing.

That line about the Mafia foot soldier is an accurate quote, by the way. Please don't think I'm pulling your leg.

Some intense political expressions involve the body, mainly in a negative way. When you "toe the party line," you speak or vote the way your party says, regardless of your own beliefs. People who are unhappy about something may decide to "vote with their feet"—a stronger version of the similar expression "take matters into their own hands." Priscilla Roberts, co-editor of a book entitled *Hong Kong in the Cold War*, described the influx of refugees in the 1950s as "Chinese who had literally voted with their feet in fleeing Communist rule." To vote with the feet often, but not always, implies emigration, whereas to "press the flesh" inevitably means to shake a serious quantity of hands. Politicians do this a lot—before an election, anyway.

The numerous English expressions involving the hand often have an underlying theme: power. If you have me in the palm of your hand, you enjoy power over me. I might acknowledge your triumph by saying, "I've got to hand it to you." To lose control of a situation is to see it get out of hand. Any type of contest will probably involve one of the participants gaining the upper hand—and, in the end, winning "hands down." In any sort of confrontation, an act that rebounds on a person, giving an opponent a better chance, "plays into their hand." These days, that expression can be found in surprising contexts. In 2015, the website eater.com published an article on the rise of Burgundy in the United States at the expense of Bordeaux, and the author stated: "America's shift toward healthier eats ultimately played into the hand of Pinot Noir and the Burgundy that is derived from it." Who knew that grapes had fingers?

 Combing the Giraffe

Speakers of Polish use an expression that, translated literally, means "We take ourselves into our fist." What are the Poles up to when they contort themselves like this?

The same as Russians who "take themselves into their hands," and Germans who "tear themselves together." If this is starting to sound familiar, it's because all three of those idioms mean basically the same as the English expressions "Pull yourself together" and "Get a grip." In every case, a mood swing or change of heart depends on the work of hands.

Do you intend to renounce a belief you once held close to your heart? Then you might want to say, "I wash my hands of it." A "knuckle sandwich" is a terrific idiom for a punch, and there's no better expression for a reprimand than a "rap across the knuckles." If I "knuckle down" to a job I've been avoiding, I may have my hands full. I might need to use some "elbow grease"—to work very hard, that is. Hopefully my left hand will know what my right hand is doing, or else my actions will be "ham-fisted." But if I'm forced to give up, the task being just too much for me, then I've reluctantly agreed to "knuckle under."

All these expressions show the physicality of English. Their body language is idiomatic. They communicate meanings born in the sense of touch.

A familiar term now undergoing a dramatic change of meaning is "shorthand." For centuries it referred only to a method of quick writing, relying on notations and symbols instead of full words and letters. Shorthand required agility with both mind and fingers; it predated the typewriter, let alone the laptop. Later, the word grew to mean any makeshift form of communication.

Today, though, you'll see it used in a much wider context. It's well on its way to replacing the word *abbreviation*, as in this line from a recent *Car and Driver* blog: "EPS, which is the typical shorthand for electric power steering." And it has also become an adjective where "symbolic" might have appeared before—a film review in the *Guardian*, for example, which described vinyl records as "Hollywood's shorthand signifier . . . for authenticity and a maverick spirit."

Words are always dying, just as words are always being born. But some words manage to escape death thanks to their presence in a flourishing idiom. They're known as fossil words. *Sleight* is a good example. Up until the seventeenth century, it was a common English term. To Shakespeare and his contemporaries, it meant craft, strategy, deceit or cleverness. Then, for no obvious reason, the word faded away—except in the familiar phrase "sleight of hand." Similarly, the adjective *bandy*, an old word for bowed or crooked, now survives only in the expression "bandy-legged."

The term *akimbo* has a different sort of history. Right from the start, six hundred years ago, it meant a particular stance: hands on hips, elbows pointing outward. The word was, so to speak, parasitic on "arms"—you'd never see or hear it except in the context of "arms akimbo." Yet in recent years "akimbo" has begun to attach itself to the back of other nouns, usually evoking something spread or bent. In August 2017, for instance, an article in *Teen Vogue* described a Manhattan party in which "half the crowd takes turns dropping to the ground in fluid succession, limbs akimbo, as they cycle through dance moves."

Akimbo is a rare word: unless you learn its meaning, the phrase "limbs akimbo" will be deeply baffling. By contrast, "cold shoulder" is an expression for disdain or rejection that makes perfect intuitive sense—it's the opposite of a warm embrace. "Cold shoulder" was, in fact, invented by the Scottish novelist Sir Walter Scott in the early nineteenth century. Scott was the most popular author of his time, and once he'd slipped the phrase into two of his books, it spread fast and wide.

The distinction between a cold shoulder and a warm heart is nothing you need search a dictionary for. As Samuel McNerney explained in a 2011 essay in *Scientific American*, "Our cognition is influenced, perhaps determined, by our experiences in the physical world. This is why we say that something is 'over our heads' to express the idea that we do not understand; we are drawing upon the physical inability to not see something over our heads and the mental feeling of uncertainty. Or why we understand warmth with affection; as infants and children, the subjective judgment of affection almost always corresponded with the sensation of warmth, thus giving way to metaphors such as 'I'm warming up to her.'"

Our experiences in the physical world include, memorably, experiences involving the sexual organs—the "private parts," as people used to say—but a lot of these expressions are offensive. I'll pass over them in silence here, merely noting that, although only men have "family jewels," both sexes can be said to possess nether regions and wobbly bits.

Household Names

Australian slang is among the richest in the English-speaking world, and it's from Down Under that the expression "pointing Percy at the porcelain" comes. Percy is the name of no particular individual but rather any and every penis, and the porcelain in question is the toilet. The idiom is an elaborate way of saying "urinate."

It may not have been invented, but it was certainly popularized, by the actor and comedian Barry Humphries. In his 1972 film *The Adventures of Barry McKenzie*, the lead character says: "Now listen, mate, I need to splash the boots. You know, strain the potatoes. Water the horses. You know, go where the big knobs hang out. Shake hands with the wife's best friend? Drain the dragon? Siphon the python? Ring the rattlesnake? You know, unbutton the mutton? Like, point Percy at the porcelain?"

As a boy, I was never quite sure where my loins were. If I'd found my way to the vast *Oxford English Dictionary*, it wouldn't have been much help. A definition given there is downright coy: "the part of the body that should be covered by clothing and about which the clothes are bound." I learned eventually that the word has a confusing double meaning. It can refer either to the entire lower torso or to the male genitals. From the first, we have the old expression "gird up your loins"—to prepare for a battle or some other exhausting effort. From the second, we have the idiom "fruit of the loins"—a child. If you want to pay tribute to the child's mother, just modify the expression and say "fruit of the womb."

What's surprising, on the face of it, is why English has a limited range of idioms for pregnancy. Sure, there are some. But the majority are a little goofy, and none of them do much to hint at the magnitude of the experience. Both "in the family way" and "with child" sound deeply old-fashioned. "Eating for two" and "bun in the oven" are among the more widely heard idioms, and they're not the only ones involving food. British English has the cheery expressions "pea in the pod" and "in the pudding club." Australians are more likely to say "up the duff," one of the meanings of duff being a steamed pudding. James Joyce used the idiom "up the pole" in his novel *Ulysses*, and that phrase still has some currency in Ireland. "Knocked up" is objectionable, while "expecting a happy event" is sentimental. All in all, it's not a great list.

This may reflect an inherent sexism in the language—a silencing, or at least a quieting, of women's perspectives. Baseball fields and battlefields have spawned more idioms than pregnancy. But maybe the idiomatic jokiness also suggests a nervousness about the experience, a desire not to tempt fate. In Renaissance Italy, it's said, most women made out a will as soon as they learned they were pregnant; in Victorian England, as many as one in every fifteen births led to the mother's death. Across most of the world at that time, the death rate for mothers and very young children was staggeringly high (in some places, it still is). Perhaps an uncertainty about the outcome—a fear of celebrating prematurely—meant that idioms for pregnancy remained scarce.

And birth itself? Apart from the pious phrase "blessed event," most English expressions referring to birth have nothing to do with the actual experience—they refer instead to some aspect of a person's life after infancy. "Born on the wrong side of the blanket" evokes illegitimacy, while "born on the wrong side of the tracks" suggests poverty. Gullible or innocent people are said to be "born yesterday." An expression that was indeed born yesterday—well, in the twenty-first century—is "birth tourism," the practice by which a woman travels to another country while heavily pregnant in hopes that the newborn will gain citizenship rights. There is, as well, the regrettable idiom "strangle at birth," meaning to stop something at a very early stage. In 2016, the governor of the Bank of England, Mark Carney, declared that innovations in financial technology "should neither be the Wild West nor strangled at birth."

Idioms make ideas spring into action. They embody our feelings. But when they're mixed as ineptly as in Carney's speech, they can sound downright ridiculous.

Run Down

Were you "born under a lucky star"? If so, one element of your good fortune is likely to be good health. You can thank your lucky stars in a host of different ways, for English is blessed with idioms that evoke physical well-being. Some of them are wry—think of "there's life in the old dog yet," or "full of beans," or "fresh as a daisy." "Consistency is the last refuge of the unimaginative," Oscar Wilde once wrote, and there's no point in asking how a dog that has dined on beans can resemble a flower, especially if its batteries have been recharged along the way. That would make for a very odd picture, nothing at all like the proverbial "picture of health."

When you're in fine fettle, your body is healthy and your spirits high—*fettle* is one of those fossil words left over from the past, like *sleight* and *bandy*. Fettles were straps or handles, but the word was never common. I suspect that "in fine fettle" is an offshoot of the baffling phrase "fit as a fiddle" (or, in the past, "fine as a fiddle"). Violins are temperamental instruments, but when they're tuned right and played well, they can set your feet to dancing. It's good to be alive and kicking, as they say, and even better to jump for joy.

Some of the expressions for good health come with a shadow of disease lurking in the background. To receive "a clean bill of health" suggests that you were facing the risk, or the reality, of sickness. "A new lease on life" is a fine thing to earn, although it indicates the old lease was running out. Even the simple expression "up and about" implies that a person has gone through a spell of being down and immobile. Something—perhaps medicine, perhaps not—has done the former patient "a world of good."

English contains plenty of expressions arising from the awareness that for mortal beings like ourselves, health doesn't last forever. Sooner or later, we'll need help. Sooner or later, we'll die. And this knowledge can be "a bitter pill to swallow." When that idiom shows up in direct connection with medical topics, the results can be awkward—in 2017, for example, a journalist writing in the *Winnipeg Free Press* complained that "closing three emergency rooms in Winnipeg is a bitter pill to swallow." But the expression is more often applied in the political realm, where it symbolizes a hurt response to almost any unpopular decision. Efforts to reduce the ensuing pain might "sweeten the bitter pill," but the pain will linger.

Or those efforts might be "just what the doctor ordered." That expression can be applied to almost any topic, and any sort of doctor will do just fine. "Given all of the negative press the *Han Solo* movie has received," a Hollywood website declared in July 2017, "this *Star Wars: The Last Jedi* behind-the-scenes footage is just what the doctor ordered." "If summer's heat has left a few holes in your garden," added a columnist for the *Columbus Dispatch*, culinary herbs "might be just what the garden doctor ordered." Back in 1954, "just what the doctor ordered" was the slogan of a promotional campaign for L&M cigarettes. Rhetorically speaking, the doctor gets around.

Doctors don't always follow their own advice, though. "Physician, heal thyself!" is a proverb that goes back to the Bible. Doctors are often said to make the worst patients—experts at diagnosing others but hopeless at treating themselves. Nor do patients always want to hear what physicians tell them. If they trust the medical information available on the internet, they may now be said to place their faith in "Doctor Google."

Doubts about the medical profession are evident in a couple of other idioms. "Spin doctor" dates from the 1980s. A *Washington Post* reporter at the time explained the phrase by saying, "The competing camps engaged in a game of persuasion and perception: 'spin doctoring,' as the craft of explaining to reporters what really happened is known in political circles." The idiom may derive from baseball, where a pitcher places spin on the ball, attempting to deceive the batter, or it may arise from the old habit of spinning a yarn. Regardless of the origin of the phrase, the masters of this dubious practice are always identified as spin doctors, not spin lawyers or spin professors.

A related art is that of "doctoring up." This phrase doesn't automatically carry a negative sense: it can fill in for the old expression "touching up," a late or small improvement made for cosmetic purposes. But "doctor up" also means to falsify the truth by concealing or altering the nature of something. As long ago as 1890, the makers of a British soap advertised their product by saying: "Vinolia Soap is not coloured, polished, whitened, made transparent with chemicals, or in any way 'doctored up.'" Fast-forward to 2016: the educator and film producer Maureen Ryan told a *Time* reporter that parents should encourage their teenage children to "look at the nuts and bolts of actual media production, and recognize how much is not real, produced with tricks . . . or doctored up in postproduction." Nurses and midwives don't attract this kind of skepticism in idioms, although it's always possible to "nurse a grievance."

The way we talk about an event affects how we think about it. In the 1970s, the psychologists Elizabeth Loftus and John Palmer demonstrated this in a famous experiment. They showed short films of traffic accidents to groups of students and then asked the students a question about how fast they thought the cars were moving. When the question stated that the cars had "contacted" one another, the students guessed the speed to be, on average, 31.8 miles an hour. But when the question spoke about the cars having "smashed" each other, the answer increased to an average of 40.5 miles an hour. The images shown to the two groups were identical, but the students' perception of speed depended not just on what they watched but on the words they read.

That kind of awareness is valuable to spin doctors and other professionals keen on doctoring things up—to an extent, political rhetoric is always an exercise in branding. And in the United States, those on the political right have showed great skill at guiding popular opinion by negative branding. In Britain, Canada, Australia and other countries, politicians and media routinely speak of the "public health system" or "publicly funded health care." But in the United States (the only wealthy nation that does not provide a form of universal health care to its citizens), a standard expression for the same concept is "socialized medicine." "Socialized" calls to mind the horrors of the Soviet Union. The widespread use of this idiom in the United States has helped to maintain a for-profit medical system.

Spoonfuls of sugar

"A spoonful of sugar helps the medicine go down" is an expression that began as the name of a song in the 1964 children's movie *Mary Poppins*—to anyone who has seen the movie, this is one idiom that cries out to be sung—and quickly became a proverb. Like so many proverbs, it can be adapted to the needs of many occasions. An exposé of medical testing, published in the *Smithsonian* in March 2017, was entitled "A Spoonful of Sugar Helps the Radioactive Oatmeal Go Down."

Other idioms involving medicine are less controversial. When a treatment succeeds, medicine will earn its nickname as the "healing art." If things go wrong, you may wish to recall a time-honored saying: "The cure is worse than the disease." The healing power of humor is implicit in the expression "Laughter is the best medicine." A "taste of her own medicine" can refer to any reprisal or retaliation, and the woman who endures this unpleasant treatment has been forced to "take her medicine."

Several other English proverbs also reflect a stoical uncertainty in the face of illness. "What can't be cured must be endured" offered cold comfort to generations of patients before the advent of antibiotics in the mid-twentieth century. "An ounce of prevention is worth a pound of cure" implies a similar absence of faith in successful treatment—it's far better to ensure you never fall ill than to become dependent on doctors. A proverb attributed to both German and British sources neatly sums up the limits of medicine: "Old age is a hospital that takes in all diseases."

For centuries, the most feared of all illnesses was the bubonic plague, an infectious bacterial disease that had no cure. It became known as the "black death" in the Middle Ages, when it killed about one-third of the population of Europe and half the population of China. Small wonder that "avoid like the plague" became a frequent expression. Its origin is somewhat incongruous. St. Jerome, an ascetic lion tamer and Bible translator of the late Roman Empire, wrote, "A clergyman who engages in business, and who rises from poverty to wealth, and from obscurity to a high position, avoid as you would the plague." You'd think there might have been rogues and villains more necessary for people to shun.

Merchant of Words

"A plague o' both your houses!" cries the young Mercutio in *Romeo and Juliet* just after suffering a mortal wound in a street brawl. Mercutio is a silver-tongued friend of Romeo, one of the Montagues, but as he feels the approach of death, he curses both them and the Capulets (Juliet's clan). The line has served as the title of a polemic about the burning of poor neighborhoods in New York, a book about minor political parties in Australia, and a mystery novel set in the Middle Ages. That's the kind of reach and resonance a few words of Shakespeare can have.

Romeo and Juliet was one of Shakespeare's earliest tragedies, and it has proved tremendously popular through the ages—the fountainhead of dozens, if not hundreds, of ballets, operas, movies, books and songs. Two other idioms that owe their life to the play are "star-crossed lovers" and "fortune's fool." Shakespeare didn't coin the expression "wild goose chase"—in his day, it referred to a complex type of horse race—but his use of the phrase in *Romeo and Juliet* made it enduringly famous.

Apart from the plague, few diseases have entered English idioms under their standard name. Cancer—the great scourge of wealthy nations today—is known only from the jocular expression "cancer stick," meaning a cigarette. A century ago, tuberculosis was both very common and greatly feared, but no idioms mention it by name. Tuberculosis is a Latin term that entered English via a German intermediary in the mid-nineteenth century, by which point it could be evoked through an assortment of dramatic phrases, including "galloping consumption," "the white disease," "the king's evil" and "the wasting disease." The ancient technical name for tuberculosis, "phthisis," is hard to spell and even harder to pronounce, and it is now understandably obscure.

There are some ailments whose names sound like idioms in their own right: scarlet fever, whooping cough, yellow fever, chickenpox. Some of these illnesses have alternative names—whooping cough is also "pertussis," for instance, and chickenpox is "varicella." But given a choice between a vivid English phrase and a technical-sounding Latin word, most people will opt for the English. It took centuries before "epilepsy" became familiar enough for the common expression "falling sickness" to be discarded. And even if "halitosis" is now widely understood, good old "bad breath" continues to flourish.

A rare condition that was diagnosed in Japan in the 1990s, before Western medicine accepted its existence, comes with the formal name of "takotsubo cardiomyopathy." *Takotsubo* is the Japanese word for a type of octopus trap, which the bulging left ventricle of patients is said to resemble. These patients have endured sudden and severe emotional stress, causing the heart muscle to weaken. But good luck in making takotsubo cardiomyopathy familiar among English speakers. Surely the affliction will be known instead by a poignant idiom: "broken heart syndrome."

Sexually transmitted diseases are often grouped together under the acronym STD—in the age of Twitter, English is bursting with acronyms. (Besides, "gonorrhea" and "chlamydia" are nearly as difficult to spell as "phthisis.") These illnesses were known in the past by picturesque names like "Cupid's itch" and "Venus's curse." A blander euphemism was "social disease." For a time, the disease that would finally be identified as HIV/AIDS—so much easier to say than "human immunodeficiency virus/acquired immune deficiency syndrome"—had the nickname "4-H disease," because in the United States its early victims were drawn mostly from the ranks of homosexuals, hemophiliacs, heroin users and Haitian immigrants. More common was the awful phrase "gay plague."

But the most memorable idiom for a sexually transmitted disease is one that involves a disturbing episode in American history, and it shows how idioms can be misused. In 1932, "colored people" in the Tuskegee area of eastern Alabama received official notices promising free treatment for "bad blood." Hundreds of men signed up, lured by statements that read: "You may feel well and still have bad blood. Come and bring all your family." The men had unwittingly joined a secret experiment conducted by the US Public Health Service, known to insiders as the "Tuskegee Study of Untreated Syphilis in the Negro Male." The men were told that they suffered from bad blood, and even as their symptoms worsened and their pain increased, the only medicines they received were placebos. The study lasted for forty years, long after penicillin and other treatments for syphilis had become available. Few of the men survived that long. "Bad blood," for them, was a fatal euphemism.

The most common afflictions we endure are colds, flus and fevers, all of which duly appear in English idioms. Fortunately, most of us never "catch our death of cold"—one of the more flagrant exaggerations in the language. "Feed a cold and starve a fever" is a morsel of folk wisdom with dubious medical validity. A fill-in-the-blanks sentence relating to the transmission of the common cold comes with better science and broader implications: "When (America) sneezes, (Canada) catches a cold" is a good example. The expression can be applied to any two partners of unequal size or power.

After long months of sleet and snow, most of us experience spring fever—and if excitement runs high, it might reach fever pitch. Boredom and confinement, however, can give us cabin fever. As for influenza, it appears in idioms only as a kind of phantom. Anybody with a case of diplomatic flu is not really sick at all; police officers develop blue flu while using pressure tactics to advance their claims; brown bottle flu is a hangover. Influenza can be a very convenient illness.

Let's suppose you're really "coming down with something." You might be "run down." You might be feeling "out of sorts."

Maybe you've simply "run out of gas"—this expression has partially replaced the earlier "out of steam." But if your symptoms get worse, you'll be "in a bad way." You might be "sick to your stomach"—the same unhappy condition as "sick as a dog" or, on occasion, sick as horses, cats, and other animals too. Let's hope your ailments don't bring you to "death's door"—make you critically ill, that is.

The question arises: How ill do you look in the eyes of your friends and family? And the answer may depend on how "off-color" you're feeling. An old expression for good health is "in the pink." But when illness or fear drains the blood from your face, you can be left "pale as a ghost" or "white as a sheet." Or you may appear "green about the gills." (For gills, read cheeks and chin.) As the great novelist Charles Dickens wrote in a letter in 1843, "I am at this moment deaf in the ears, hoarse in the throat, red in the nose, green in the gills . . . and fractious in the temper from a most intolerable and oppressive cold." All these color-related idioms date from a period before the cities of Britain had been transformed by large-scale immigration, and before Britain and, later, the United States had planted their language all over the globe. Do "in the pink" and "white as a sheet" make sense to speakers of English in Trinidad, Pakistan, Zambia or the Philippines? Perhaps new color-related idioms will emerge from there.

One idiom seems unlikely for people of any ancestry: when you're feeling angry about something, you can argue until you're "blue in the face."

Household Names

It used to be clear who "the sick man of Europe" was: Turkey. Or more particularly, the Ottoman Empire during the second half of the nineteenth century and the first years of the twentieth. This evocative idiom dates back to an era when Turkey's economy appeared weak, its society fractured, its government lethargic. Tsar Nicholas of Russia, speaking to the British ambassador in 1853, expressed his anxiety about what would happen "when the sick man dies." The idiom spread fast. Just seven years later, an American politician named Samuel Cox recorded the following exchange in Congress: "'Mexico is our "sick man".' 'Yes; she is to America what Turkey is to Europe.'"

Journalists and commentators have found the expression too good not to use—endlessly. Since 2000 it has been applied to Britain, Spain, Germany, Russia, Italy, Greece, Portugal, France, Finland, and the entire European Union. You can bet good money that the next time a European nation faces an economic or political crisis, that nation will be identified as the sick man of Europe. The idiom also traveled east: a century ago, China was often called "the sick man of Asia." Would anyone say this now?

Irritation, annoyance, rage: the language conveys these feelings by finding physical symptoms to express emotional states of mind. To native speakers of English, the underlying meanings are clear even if, on a literal level, the idioms sound almost ludicrous. "Pain in the neck" is an example. It doesn't refer to actual stiffness or swelling, but to a particularly annoying person. (There's little difference between a pain in the neck and a pain in the ass.) You might be "sick and tired" of that person, even though you're neither ill nor exhausted. You might be "hot under the collar"—and also shirtless. Or you might be "fed up to the back teeth," an idiom that has nothing to do with either food or dentistry, but rather suggests enormous displeasure. In that event, you've probably "reached the end of your tether"—a tether being a rope for binding farm animals.

Idioms for fatigue are terse. Let's hope you're not dead on your feet. If you are, you'll be ready to drop. You're dog tired. You're all in. You're worn-out.

English can be a cruel language. Many of its expressions are callous and brutally direct. As a result, you may occasionally need to make a quick decision about using idioms that have provoked discomfort and controversy. Sometimes they involve color. Consider the negative tone of "blackmail," "black market," "blackball," "black eye" and "black mark." Other cases involve the absence of sight: "blind alley," "blind faith," "blind spot," "blind drunk," and so on. Such phrases act as a kind of poetic shorthand—without them, the language would be impoverished. Yet some people living with vision loss would like these idioms to be dropped from regular use. In response to their concerns, the Philosophy of Science Association in the United States decided to abandon the phrase "blind review."

On a case-by-case basis, some idioms are surely more objectionable than others. The saying "There's none so blind as those who will not see" is directed not at the sightless but at sighted people who are so willfully stubborn that they ignore the truth. "Blind as a bat," by contrast, offers a scornful equation of humans with small, unloved animals and is just plain wrong (no species of bat is blind, and some bats enjoy better vision than humans). Yet it's hard to imagine the language without that expression. As for "the blind leading the blind," not only is it the name of a Pieter Bruegel painting and a Mick Jagger song, it's also an image that appears in two Biblical gospels, works by several of the finest authors from ancient Rome and Greece, the canon of Buddhist scriptures, and one of the most beautiful Hindu Upanishads, composed well over two thousand years ago. Few other idioms are so deeply entrenched in human culture.

The same issues arise with expressions involving deafness. "There's none so deaf as those who will not hear" means exactly the same thing as its counterpart line about blindness. "Deaf as a post" (or a stone, nail or door) is an equivalent of "blind as a bat." But the expression "turn a deaf ear"—like "turn a blind eye"— can be taken as ascribing blame to those who have no choice in the matter.

Combing the Giraffe

It may be disconcerting to think of American Sign Language as a source of foreign expressions, but ASL, as much as any spoken language, has the ability to generate rich metaphorical idioms. Deafness is no barrier to the imagination. So, for example, a particular set of hand movements, accompanied by either puffed cheeks or a blank stare, delivers the literal meaning "train gone"—and the idiomatic sense of "missed the boat." A different set of hand gestures goes with widened eyes, producing the literal "swallowed the fish" while conveying an impression of gullibility. Perhaps this idiom in ASL drew from the English phrase "hook, line and sinker."

"Emotional cripple." "Lame duck." "Lame joke." At times, like I said, English shows no mercy.

"Social disease" and "bad blood" are euphemisms—the use of a mild or indirect expression to replace a more direct and accurate term. Some euphemisms originate in news stories and then become idioms, at least for a short period. For example, when journalists asked why US senator Mark Sanford had been missing for almost a week in 2009, his staff explained he was "hiking the Appalachian Trail." It turned out that Sanford had actually been holed up in Buenos Aires with his Argentinian mistress. For the next year or two, "hiking the Appalachian Trail" was a widely used euphemism for infidelity. But as Sanford's affair slipped from public consciousness, the idiom faded along with it. Expressions that are not tied to a single news story tend to have a much longer life.

Think of idioms like "a screw loose" and "bats in the belfry." (A belfry is an old word for a church tower containing large bells.) They've been around for a century or two, and they can still be used as euphemisms for mental illness. "Sick puppy" is a very mild euphemism for someone who behaves in a depraved, sadistic way. Its meaning has changed dramatically over time. A century ago, it evoked nobody more crazed than a lovesick admirer. In 1911, a newspaper in Indianapolis quoted a police officer as saying, "When a noted actress is in town, lots of times some poor fool, wearing a carnation in his coat lapel, will whine around after her like a sick puppy." Today, alas, he would do a lot more than whine.

Other euphemisms for—at the very least—eccentric views and odd behavior include "out to lunch," "up a tree," "cracking up" and "off his rocker." My favorite expression of this kind comes from the Australian outback: "kangaroo loose in the top paddock." But the humor in many of these idioms seems like whistling in the dark (feigning fearlessness, that is). The idioms evoking mental illness often minimize its gravity. It's as if by reducing the paralyzing impact of anxiety to nothing worse than "the heebie-jeebies," we could lessen the anxiety itself.

Most idioms for depression convey a sense of going down or getting trapped. When you're depressed, you're "in the pits," "down in the dumps," or merely "down in the mouth." You could also say "I'm in the doldrums," referring to the paralysis of a sailboat on a windless day or, more specifically, to the equatorial region of the Pacific and Atlantic Oceans where sailing vessels could drift slowly for weeks at a time, unable to escape. (Today geographers don't talk about the doldrums but rather the Intertropical Convergence Zone.) Or you could be "feeling the blues." Music is not the source of this expression—the sadness (implicit or explicit) in early-twentieth-century songs by black Americans caused the genre to be named after the idiom, one that goes much further back in time. In 1741, the English actor David Garrick had said in a letter: "I am far from being quite well, tho not troubled with the Blews as I have been." They were known as the "blue devils," too.

To drive someone round the bend has nothing to do with directing a car, truck, bus or even horse. "Round the bend" was a naval term for madness—or so it's said. The origins of this phrase are puzzling, for there are no bends on the open water. But maybe that's the whole point. People who've been driven around some imaginary bend could also be described as having "lost their marbles": gone mad, that is. "Mother was studying me with real concern," says the narrator of Saul Bellow's novel *More Die of Heartbreak*, "as if I had lost my marbles." Most linguists believe the phrase comes directly from the childhood game of marbles, but it's also possible that it adapts the French word *meubles*, meaning furniture or possessions.

Other expressions for mental illness are not euphemistic at

all—they convey a little of the terrifying power of the disease. "Foaming at the mouth" suggests a rage so extreme, it creates symptoms like those of epilepsy. "Sick at heart" is another idiom in which the literal sense and the figurative meaning stand at odds with each other. As for "nervous wreck," it's such a common phrase that we seldom pause to consider the ruin it evokes. "Out of his mind," by contrast, is direct and stark.

Out of our minds or fully inside them, we all face an eventual death sentence—not that we like to admit the fact. Even more than physical and mental illness, death provokes fear. And where fear stalks the imagination, euphemisms are sure to follow.

Check the obituaries on the websites of "funeral homes"—a euphemism in its own right. Such and such a person has "passed away," or "passed on," or merely "passed." Such and such a person has "fallen asleep," while another "has entered eternal rest." In North America, it's becoming rare to find an obituary that clearly states a person has died.

Merchant of Words

When Tom Petty and the Heartbreakers played a concert in Chicago in June 2017, a reviewer for the music website Uproxx was ecstatic. He hailed Petty as a "great American institution" and "one of those rare artists that has transcended both genre and generation." Indeed, the reviewer said, "His music will live on long past the point he's shuffled off this mortal coil."

This elaborate way of saying "died" goes back to one of the most famous speeches in all of Shakespeare: the "To be or not to be" soliloquy in *Hamlet*. Agonizing about suicide, the prince declares: "What dreams may come, / When we have shuffled off this mortal coil, / Must give us pause." In Shakespeare's day, "coil" meant bustle, confusion or turmoil—but the expression also works with the modern meaning of coil as a continuous loop or set of spirals. A mere three months after the Chicago concert, Petty died.

The plethora of euphemisms that enable us to avoid saying "died" inspired one of the funniest and most famous of all comic scenes. The "Dead Parrot sketch," as it's usually known, was broadcast on the BBC-TV show *Monty Python's Flying Circus* in 1969, featuring Michael Palin as a pet-shop owner and John Cleese as a frustrated customer trying to return a lifeless Norwegian parrot. Palin suggests the bird is simply "pining for the fjords." With growing irritability, Cleese unleashes a string of euphemisms that make it clear his bird is no longer capable of pining for anything, from pushing up the daisies and kicking the bucket to shuffling off the mortal coil and joining the choir invisible. (I love the idea of a dead parrot squawking in an unseen choir.)

Cleese omitted to say that the parrot had also pegged out, bought the farm, given up the ghost, been laid out in lavender, worn a pine overcoat, and gone to the big pet shop in the sky. Nonetheless, it was indeed an ex-parrot. In the years after the sketch was aired, the familiar idiom "sick as a dog" faced a new rival: "sick as a parrot."

The presence or approach of death often brings on the kind of dark, bitter jokes that go by the name "gallows humor." (The gallows, of course, was a structure used for hanging people.) "Over my dead body!" is a jovial way of saying "Never!" although once it was a forceful statement of defiance. If you "know where the bodies are buried," you have confidential information that might serve you well in the future. Will you make use of this knowledge? "It's your funeral"—meaning that if you do, you'll have to face the consequences.

English is particularly well stocked with idioms about bones. "I make no bones about it," you might say if your decision is clear and unhesitating. Why should bones enter into the affair? In medieval times, cooked dishes were often full of bones, and to "find a bone" is an ancient expression for encountering some difficulty. Even now, if you have "a bone to pick" with someone, that someone is giving you problems. To "find no bones," by contrast, implies an absence of complications. Over the centuries, *finding* no bones turned into *making* no bones.

Donkey's Hind Leg

"Dead as a doornail" has been traced back to the fourteenth century. It's unclear what distinguished a nail in a medieval door from any other type of nail. Had it been flattened on the inside after hammering so that it could never be pulled out and reused? This phrase has endured while other, similar expressions have retreated—people in past centuries, if their minds weren't occupied by doornails, also said "dead as a herring" and "dead as mutton." Eventually the fish and sheep were dropped in favor of the dodo, a big flightless bird from the island of Mauritius in the Indian Ocean—dodos went extinct in the 1660s, the first widely known example of human beings exterminating a whole species. Thanks to the bird's appearance in Lewis Carroll's *Alice's Adventures in Wonderland*, "dead as a dodo" became a popular expression.

A morbidly thin person can be called "a bag of bones," or "nothing but skin and bones." Hospitals and cemeteries are sometimes known as "bone factories." "A skeleton at the feast" is someone whose dark mood, or mere presence, affects the happiness of others. But if you have "a skeleton in the closet," you're guarding a shameful secret, one that could destroy your own happiness. That kind of secret can be the kiss of death for any relationship.

In the Western world, death is often personified as the Grim

Reaper. He was a terrifying figure to the inhabitants of religious, preindustrial societies—nobody you'd want to joke about. He stood poised to strike you down at any moment. But in our culture, for better or worse, people are willing to make a joke of anything, death included. And so Grim Reaper has become the name or nickname of a National Hockey League enforcer, an American professional wrestler, a couple of military air squadrons, a pair of outlaw motorcycle gangs, a Marvel Comics villain, a British heavy metal band, and at least three movies. Having started off as a much-feared threat, the Grim Reaper turned into a euphemism and is now well on his way to becoming a cliché.

Let's bring down the curtain with Shakespeare. "If I must die," says Claudio in *Measure for Measure*, "I will encounter darkness as a bride, / And hug it in mine arms."

Shooting the Breeze

We all grumble about the weather. If it's not too hot, it's too cold. If it's not too wet, it's too dry. The job of a weather forecaster is to explain what's going on now and announce what's likely to happen in the future, and dozens of weather-related idioms perform a similar task. Channeling our discontent, they use the actions of the changing sky to interpret and predict behavior.

What those idioms show is a stoicism verging on pessimism, not just about the world outside our doors but also about the world inside our minds and hearts. You might think this has something to do with the damp and changeable weather of the British Isles, the original home of the English language, and perhaps it does. But many American idioms are equally miserable.

Think of being "under the weather." It means to feel less than your best—not seriously ill, but not feeling great, either. That's an Americanism from the nineteenth century. A "weather bomb" is a newer expression from the United States for a severe storm, especially one in winter. In Britain, to "make heavy weather" of a job is to have serious or unexpected difficulty with it. The phrase is similar in meaning to "hit rough weather." Both idioms are often deployed in the business realm as a way of making economic trends and concepts seem more natural than they really are. In November 2016, for example, a website for professional investors observed that "Airline stocks have hit rough weather with a plethora of issues affecting the sector."

But, as we all know, the weather never stays the same. Eventually the sky clears and the ground dries. And then we're stuck with—well, in the world of idioms, we're stuck with "fair-weather friends": people you can't depend on. A fair-weather friend is somebody not to be trusted, somebody who will abandon you in times of need. To avoid such letdowns, we might, as an old English proverb says, "make hay while the sun shines." It advises us not to lose any time or miss any opportunities, for they might not come our way again. Seize the moment: it would be foolish to rely on the sun.

Of course, that's not what politicians say when they're on the threshold of power. On the night of his election as Canadian prime minister in 2015, Justin Trudeau declared: "Sunny ways, my friends. Sunny ways. This is what positive politics can do." Nine years earlier, David Cameron, addressing a British Conservative Party conference for the first time as party leader, famously said, "Let sunshine win the day." And in the United States, Donald Trump compared his country and perhaps himself to the sun in his 2017 inauguration speech: "We do not seek to impose our way of life on anyone, but rather to let it shine as an example. We will shine for everyone to follow." Trump's words were an echo, no doubt unconscious, of Louis XIV, the longest-serving of all French monarchs, widely known as the Sun King.

Combing the Giraffe

The Kazakh language of central Asia has a beautiful expression to show praise and gratitude for another person. If you want to thank someone just for being himself, or to tell a person how much you owe her, you would say, "I see the sun on your back."

A less exalted idiom comes from the Spanish of Argentina: "to live on a cloud of farts." If this is where you spend your time, you're sadly out of touch with the world beneath your feet. But, it must be admitted, you are not out of gas.

Metaphorically speaking, sunlight gets all the good press, and darkness the bad. Once you've risen and shone, you might be able to brighten up the day for your friends and family, and even act as a ray of hope in our increasingly dysfunctional world. I'm "blue-skying" here, of course—that is, I'm trying to break free from conventional ways of thinking. Even so, I hope that all these phrases, appearing in a book about idioms, don't strike you as coming out of the blue.

The eternal battle between optimists and pessimists can be seen in the way English treats clouds. Optimists can take heart from the saying "Every cloud has a silver lining." In other words, something good will emerge from any disaster. A popular but long-forgotten Irish novel from 1840, *Marian, or A Young Maid's Fortunes*, by Anna Maria Hall, established the phrase: "There's a silver lining to every cloud that sails about the heavens if we could only see it." Nothing is as bad as it seems.

"Cloud nine"—a dreamy state of happiness—first appeared in the United States during the 1950s. The phrase showed up at almost the same time as "cloud seven," which means the same thing. Perhaps "cloud seven" was a reference to being in seventh heaven, the highest realm of all, an ancient image in both Jewish and Muslim conceptions of the supernatural. But if so, why would "cloud eight" have entered American English a generation earlier than both "cloud seven" and "cloud nine"? A glossary of underworld English published in 1935 explains "cloud eight" as an idiom for being blissfully drunk. Maybe clouds of smoke were involved as well. Whatever the exact number, this is a cloud to be welcomed, not feared.

But then there are all the other, less pleasant types of cloud, the ones that pessimists can't help observing. You're under a cloud of suspicion—or sometimes just "under a cloud"—when other people believe you've done something wrong, even if they can't prove it. A 2016 Olympic Games report in the *Washington Post* featured the headline "Competing Under a Cloud of Suspicion, Russian Athletes Hear Boos in Rio." When there's a cloud on the horizon, expect trouble ahead. The sunny ways won't last. If you assume the opposite, you must have your head in the clouds.

Spoonfuls of sugar

In March 2017, an audience member on a BBC-TV show charged that the British government was living "in cloud-cuckoo-land" by assuming it can quit the European Union and then achieve a better trade deal. His phrase can refer to a belief in any impossible or unrealistic dream. It dates from an 1824 translation of *The Birds*, a comedy by the ancient Greek playwright Aristophanes. He imagined a city in the sky, constructed by birds, that would enable them to lord it over human beings. The translator gave this nonexistent realm the memorable name "cloud-cuckoo-land."

Clouds bring rain, but that's not necessarily a bad thing. The phrase "dry spell" evokes a drought, a period of low activity, an uncreative time. That's an American expression, whereas "right as rain" comes from Britain. If something is right as rain, there's no problem at all. Perhaps the expression arose because in much of Britain and Ireland, rain is a kind of default weather.

But give the pessimists their due. Sour idioms about rainfall are a lot more common than sweet ones. "It never rains but it pours" is a good example. You'd be entitled to say this on a morning when you left a painful root-canal procedure in a car that promptly broke down, requiring a hefty payment to a towing company and making you late for a job you're at risk of losing. In that event, it's to be hoped you managed to save for a rainy day—a time of trouble, that is. Life may have a habit of spoiling your plans, ruining your hopes, and generally "raining on your parade." This last phrase is a young one, as idioms go: "Don't Rain on My Parade" was a song made famous by Barbra Streisand in the 1964 Broadway musical *Funny Girl*.

One of the most complex phrases relating to weather is "Take a rain check." It began in the language of baseball in the late nineteenth century. When a game was called off because of bad weather, a spectator who had paid to attend would be given a rain check: a ticket or token that could be redeemed sometime in the future. Soon the phrase began to apply to indoor events, too. In 1917, a concert promoter stated in the magazine *Vanity Fair* that if "you discover that your bronchial condition is beyond your control . . . we will gladly give you a rain-check." Later, the expression grew to mean a store's solemn promise to deliver currently unavailable goods. But those promises couldn't always be trusted: sometimes the goods would never materialize. And today, when you ask for a rain check, you're indicating that you don't want to do something, certainly not now, maybe never. "I'll take a rain check" has become an oblique way of saying no.

So much for metaphorical rain. There's also the physical kind that it's impossible to avoid, the sort of moisture that leaves you soaking wet if you're outside for even a minute. That's when, it's often said, "the heavens open." You might also say it's "raining buckets." As an old joke puts it, the only thing worse than raining buckets is hailing taxis.

Tomatoes on Your Eyes

When the heavens open and it rains buckets, we might also say "It's raining cats and dogs." This is a timeworn phrase, more than three hundred years old, and it may have something to do with the traditional hostility between dogs and cats. But an even older usage—recorded about 1630 in a play by an obscure London dramatist named Richard Brome—evoked a rain of polecats and dogs. Polecats are widespread carnivores, often foul-smelling, the ancestor of the domesticated ferret. You don't find them prowling the clouds.

Violent weather conditions such as tornado waterspouts have led to very occasional falls of frogs and fish from the sky, but there are no attested records of cats, dogs or polecats dropping out of thin air. In many languages, though, heavy rain is the subject of a peculiar idiom.

The Welsh talk about it "raining old ladies and sticks"; in Dutch, it can "rain kittens, old wives or pipe stems"; and in Danish, it "rains shoemakers' apprentices." That may be even harder to explain than a Spanish idiom that is said to be common in Medellín, Colombia: "It's raining husbands."

Once the downpour finally stops and the sun peers out from the clouds, a rainbow might appear in the sky. Rainbows can look magical, and their arrival at the end of a storm makes them a perennial symbol of hope. The earliest example of this may be the aftermath of the great flood in Genesis, where a rainbow served as proof of a new covenant between God and all life on Earth. One of the great slave songs among African Americans put a sardonic spin on this idea: "God gave Noah the rainbow sign, / No more water, the fire next time." So much for easy hope. The proverbial "pot of gold at the end of the rainbow"— an image that goes back to pre-Christian Ireland—evokes both great wealth and the impossibility of achieving it. Likewise, anyone who's purported to be "chasing rainbows" is trying to attain the impossible.

Rainbows took on a political meaning in the late twentieth century. Archbishop Desmond Tutu, a leader in the fight against apartheid, coined the phrase "rainbow nation" to describe a South Africa in which people of all colors and ethnicities would feel at home. "All the colors of the rainbow" has become not just a description of the splintering of sunlight but an idiom for diversity—sexual diversity, in particular. The link between rainbows and the LGBTQ movement owes a lot to Judy Garland, a gay icon who sang "Over the Rainbow," a song that imagines a new world "where the clouds are far behind me," in *The Wizard of Oz*. The unofficial emblem of the LGBTQ movement, the rainbow flag, features six colored stripes of equal size.

Some LGBTQ activists in recent years have "thrown caution to the winds"—that is, they have been daring and even reckless in pursuing their goals. In the late nineteenth century, the preferred version of the idiom was "throw discretion to the winds." Either way, the winds in question are those of fortune. They are unpredictable—you can't be sure of their speed or direction. As the eighty-seven-year-old actor William Shatner remarked in an interview with the Albany *Times Union* in March 2018, "We're all under the illusion that we have some control over our life, but we're really buffeted by all kinds of errant winds of fortune." That was so when Shatner played Captain Kirk on the original *Star Trek*, and it has remained so ever since.

Winds and breezes enjoy a good reputation in English idioms. Britain was a sailing nation, and it's bad for any sailing vessel to lie becalmed, unable to move. But the wind must always be given due respect. Out on the waves, you can never take a wind for granted. "Sailing close to the wind" means doing something dangerous or unlawful, something you'll only just get away with. To "get wind of something" is to learn about it in advance—and having done so, you'll sense which way the wind is blowing.

The power of fast-moving air is evident in old phrases like "spit against the wind" and "speak to the wind," both of them elaborate ways of expressing futility. As for "the winds of change," seldom if ever can they be resisted.

Just as every cloud is supposed to have a silver lining, so too can we say "It's an ill wind that blows nobody good." In all likelihood, this is another sailing idiom, and an ancient one. Shakespeare adapted it in his early play *Henry VI, Part Three*, when a man drags onto the stage the body of an opponent he has defeated in battle. "Ill blows the wind that profits nobody," he says. The twist of the knife comes a few lines later, when the speaker stops to look at the dead man's face—and realizes he has killed his own father.

Soft, harmless movements of air are known as breezes, and they appear in a few relaxed expressions. To "shoot the breeze" is to engage in idle, unthreatening talk. If a job is easy to do, we say "It's a breeze"—a meteorological version of "It's easy as pie." Likewise, when you breeze through an exam, the questions you answered were a piece of cake. Only the expression "twist in the breeze" carries a darker undercurrent of suspense and uncertainty. Early in 2017, a website devoted to professional baseball said of a Blue Jays slugger that "José Bautista has spent the entire offseason twisting in the breeze."

The seriousness that lies behind that phrase means that, more often than not, it's uttered about the wind instead of the breeze. "Time to Let Toronto Twist in the Wind": that was the headline a *Toronto Star* editor placed above a letter suggesting that taxpayers outside the city should not be forced to bail Toronto out. Breezy or windy, the two expressions evoke not only laundry but also execution by hanging. Their meaning is similar to that of another idiom: "left hung out to dry."

If life or work is hurling more at you than you can easily cope with, and if you're struggling to find the way ahead, you might say you're "snowed under." This phrase evokes a wild blizzard—winter at its most perilous and least predictable. The idea of being snowed under may have been the reason that, during the Second World War, American soldiers began to talk about a "snow job"—a sustained attempt to deceive people by bombarding them with insincere or inaccurate words. But surprisingly, other idioms involving snow are more concerned with the color and purity of the substance than with the dangers it can bring.

Think of the familiar adjective "snow-white." Nearly a thousand years before Walt Disney made an animated movie about seven dwarfs and a spirited girl, it was an idiom for absolute whiteness. "Snow on the roof" and "snow on the mountain" are both expressions referring to a person's white hair. (I would have said "lighthearted" expressions, but "light-headed" seems more to the point.) "Pure as the driven snow" is a very old phrase for chastity or moral virtue, while "snow bunny" is a much younger idiom, meaning either a novice at skiing or a young woman at a ski resort.

In linguistic terms, ice is more dangerous than snow. There's the proverbial "tip of the iceberg," to begin with. Almost 90 percent of the mass of any iceberg lies under the surface, making icebergs much larger than they appear. The *Titanic* sank to its watery grave in 1912, and after the disaster, the phrase "tip of the iceberg" became both more common and more threatening in tone. Being "on thin ice" evokes an immediate sense of menace. "Ice maiden" is a dismissive term for a woman who controls her emotions well and shows little feeling. And to "put on ice" is to postpone a decision or delay an action until some point in the future.

The American playwright Eugene O'Neill gave a metaphorical twist to the meaning of ice in one of his most famous plays, *The Iceman Cometh*. The play is set in 1912, long before most American homes had refrigeration, a time when both ice and milk would be delivered door to door. One of the main characters in the drama tells a story about his wife having an affair with the iceman—but, like most of O'Neill's works, *The Iceman Cometh* is a tragedy, and the iceman ultimately becomes a symbol of death.

"Break the ice," by contrast, means to take action, often in a positive sense. A jewelry company named Sequin once invited a few editors of the powerful fashion magazine *Vogue* to visit its Manhattan showroom. At first the meeting did not go well, and the editors from *Vogue* remained silent. "They were very nice, but they were nonreactive," Kim Dryer, one of the owners of Sequin, told the *New York Times*. "Then the rabbit hopped across the room, and it broke the ice completely. It changed the dynamic of the whole meeting." The icebreaker was a pet black rabbit named Grizzly, not a wild rabbit trying to reach Central Park.

Donkey's Hind Leg

The British have an idiom for doing something pointless and unnecessary: "taking coals to Newcastle." Because the city of Newcastle was built on a rich seam of coal, the last thing it needed was imported fuel. The idiom has outlasted the fuel, for present-day Britain has no deep coal mines and uses little coal of any kind.

In the United States, an idiom emerged with a similar meaning: "selling ice to Eskimos." Anyone who could make such a ridiculous deal would be a master of salescraft, and so the phrase can be spoken in either an admiring or a critical tone. In Canada over the past few decades, the word *Inuit* has almost entirely replaced *Eskimos* (the professional football team in Edmonton being the sole exception), and the expression "selling ice to Eskimos" has fallen out of use.

Extremes of temperature fare poorly in idioms. A day of bitter chill is a day when it's "cold enough to freeze the balls off a brass monkey"—one of the most picturesque of all idioms. In some parts of the English-speaking world, people say "brass monkey weather" to mean a spell of bitter cold. But what of the weather in your heart? If something "leaves you cold," it has no effect on you—and if someone offers you "cold comfort," you're receiving no support at all. Stella Gibbons used this expression in the title of one of the best-selling British novels of the 1930s, a satire of rural life entitled *Cold Comfort Farm*. English doesn't have any expressions about hot shoulders and hot comfort, but it does warn against getting "hot under the collar." Both that expression and a similar one, "hot and bothered," evoke a high level of agitation. Be careful not to get into "hot water"—into serious trouble, that is.

What the language prefers is warmth. To warm up to somebody or something is to overcome an initial dislike. The phrase "warm-blooded"—when it's not merely a scientific description of mammals and birds—implies the presence of robust emotion without the negative side effects of being hot-blooded and the even worse connotations of cold-blooded. Admittedly you don't want to look like death warmed up (or "death warmed over")—death trumps warmth, so to speak, just like it trumps everything else. But if you're cozy and snug on a bitter day, then you'll also be "warm as toast," and you'll probably have a warm and fuzzy feeling in your heart.

It's good to *feel* warm. It's equally desirable to *be* cool—a word with an immensely complex history. Being "cool as a cucumber" has implied steadiness and self-possession since the eighteenth century. Gradually the negative associations ("She was cool to the idea") began to lose out to the positive ones ("He's a cool customer"). But it remains a word in flux.

The seasons, like day-to-day weather, can serve as metaphors for stages in a human life. Many languages, including English, associate spring with youth, joy and renewal; summer with rest and pleasure; autumn with decline and age; winter with death. Each season can symbolize a set of emotions. All this was summed up by the Baroque composer Antonio Vivaldi in his brilliant sequence of four violin concerti, *The Four Seasons*. In the first movement of Summer, for example, he stated that the music should evoke "languor caused by the heat." The changing moods expressed by music suggest the flow of time through the course of a year. It's fortunate for music lovers that Vivaldi didn't live in a climate where the only seasons are "the Wet" and "the Dry"—or in a climate where there are no seasons at all.

Merchant of Words

"Shall I compare thee to a summer's day?" Shakespeare wrote in one of his best-loved sonnets. The short answer would have been "Not really," but it took him much of the poem to reach that point. "Sometime too hot the eye of heaven shines": you can't expect perfect weather, even in July. The recipient of the poem casts even a summer day into shadow: "Thou art more lovely and more temperate." Fine weather will eventually turn into rain but, on the strength of this sonnet, "Thy eternal summer shall not fade." In praising the grace and beauty of his beloved, Shakespeare also signaled his faith in his own powers as a writer.

One of the most mysterious weather-related expressions is "Indian summer," a stretch of clear and warm days in the fall. The idiom dates from 1778, when the writer Hector St. John de Crèvecoeur used it in rural New York to mean "a short interval of smoke and mildness" before winter. The expression is a New World adaptation of an Old World idea. In past centuries, a period of sunlight and warmth in mid-October was known to the British as "little summer of St. Luke" (the Gospel writer whose feast day was celebrated at that time). Speakers of German depict the same weather less reverently: "old wives' summer."

So why "Indian summer"? Was it a slur on indigenous peoples, this kind of graceful weather holding out a promise that would soon prove deceptive? More positively, did it allude to the harvest season among the Iroquois, or to a period when fires were set in the fields? Or did settlers coin the phrase to mean a time of peace, when raids had ended for the year? There is, as yet, no consensus.

Whatever the answer, the idiom has spread throughout the English-speaking world, and today it can be used in any context to refer to a late flowering. In 2017, the London newspaper the *Independent* ran an article about the tennis hero Roger Federer, by then thirty-five years old but again winning major tournaments, that stated: "Federer's Indian summer continues apace."

Some of the most vivid of all idioms involving weather are the ones that evoke violent storms. Here again, the sky functions as a prime source of expressions to describe people: their actions, their behavior, their moods. If someone looks like thunder or has a face like thunder, their anger is all too obvious. "A storm is brewing" when trouble is still some distance off. Even if everything is peaceable for the moment, it may only be "the calm before the storm." In October 2017, Donald Trump quoted this expression to reporters at the White House. Asked what the storm would be, he replied, "You'll find out."

Spoonfuls of sugar

"You stole my thunder!" Unless you're Thor, that can't be a serious accusation. For mortals, it means you took someone else's words or ideas and used them for your own advantage. The idiom has a clear origin. In 1709, a London dramatist and critic named John Dennis invented a new way of mimicking the sound of thunder for his play *Appius and Virginia*. The thunder method was successful, but the play was not; it closed after a few days. Attending a production of *Macbeth* soon after, Dennis was startled to find his noisemaking apparatus back in use. "Damn them!" he said. "They will not let my play run, but they steal my thunder."

It's always possible, of course, that a political or economic storm will "blow over" and be soon forgotten. With hindsight, we might even recognize it as a "tempest in a teapot"—a marvelously

evocative idiom that can be traced back to the Roman states-
man and author Cicero, writing more than two millennia ago.
"Gratidius raised a tempest in a ladle, as the saying is," Cicero
observed. The idiom spread and took root all over Europe and
far beyond. Today, speakers of German and French downplay a
"storm in a glass of water," speakers of Arabic and Bengali dismiss
a "storm in a cup," and speakers of Korean devalue a "typhoon
in a teacup," but the meaning in all languages remains the same.

Back to serious quantities of wind and rain. "Any port in a
storm" suggests that when things are tough, some kind of help
is always welcome. If you find refuge from whatever's menac-
ing you, then you've been able to "weather the storm." To "take
something by storm" is to be rapidly and overwhelmingly successful, even to the point of coming as a "bolt from the blue."
That idiom suggests extreme surprise, whereas the expressions
"lightning fast" and "greased lightning" suggest extreme speed.
The word *greased* serves merely to exaggerate or intensify an idea
already present in *lightning*.

Another American expression, "lightning in a bottle," com-
bines the notions of speed and improbability, evoking an achievement that would be not only quick but also unlikely. The *Globe
and Mail*'s review of a 2017 movie about the life of novelist J. D.
Salinger carried the headline "*Rebel in the Rye* Fails to Capture
Lightning in a Bottle." A phrase with a less obvious origin in
the skies is "blue streak." When somebody talks or swears a blue
streak, the words are pouring out fast—and profanely. Just like
lightning, words can be dangerous.

Many people associate the phrase "perfect storm" with Sebastian Junger's 1997 book and the Hollywood movie *The Perfect Storm* that was made a few years later. In meteorological terms, a perfect storm is a violent event that forms when two or three weather systems clash with enormous destructive force. The phrase had, in fact, been around for a few centuries before Junger's book appeared, but his account of a fatal storm in the North Atlantic made it famous overnight. It had become almost a cliché by 2007, when it appeared on an annual list of overused expressions. But the global financial crisis and the political turmoil of the last few years have kept the expression "perfect storm" very much alive.

One of the most urgent and difficult challenges of our time is climate change—a clear and present threat to the world as we know it, for humans and for thousands of the animal species we share the planet with. In the past few years, a number of expressions about climate change have become familiar currency.

Between the 1980s and the early 2000s, the most commonly heard phrase to describe climate change was "global warming." It seemed like a good way to express the results of what was often described as a rise in "the greenhouse effect." Nobody disputes the existence of this effect—the natural process by which radiation from Earth's atmosphere raises the planet's surface temperature above what it would be without an atmosphere—and scientists no longer need to debate whether the greenhouse effect has been enhanced by human beings pumping ever higher levels of carbon dioxide into the air.

A problem with "global warming," though, is that the expression has a comfortable, reassuring tone. In northern countries like Canada, some people think it sounds highly desirable. Apart from all the happy associations that come with the feeling of warmth, "global warming" is also a profoundly inaccurate phrase, for climate change is not consistent—certain regions are heating up more dramatically than others, and the effects of climate change include not just a rise in temperature but also an increase in droughts and violent storms. To avoid minimizing the impacts of climate change, many scientists now avoid the expression "global warming," or use it much less than they did a decade ago. The British author and activist George Monbiot has suggested that even "climate change" underplays the seriousness of the issue. Monbiot would prefer us to talk about "climate breakdown."

The prospect of people abandoning their homes because of drought, crop failures, rising sea levels, storm surges and other events has led to the emergence of a new idiom: "climate refugee." Again, this is a contested expression. Some people prefer the phrase "environmental migrant." The residents of the Carteret Islands, off the coast of Papua New Guinea, became climate refugees after 2006 when they began to be evacuated from their low-lying, flood-prone homeland; the entire population is expected to leave within the next few years. Farmers who have given up trying to survive off the parched soil of Somalia, Kenya, Ethiopia and other African nations are also climate refugees.

The reason behind these kinds of displacements has to do

with what's now being called our "carbon addiction." Every one of us has a "carbon footprint," an idiom first used in the late 1990s as a measure of an individual's total carbon emissions and the environmental impact they cause. Each nation has a carbon footprint, too. An article in *Salon* sounded a rare note of optimism when it stated, "All the right things came together in 2016 for the United States to shrink its carbon footprint in some dramatic and record-breaking ways."

As the effects of climate change continue to worsen, new expressions emerge out of a need to describe and interpret what's going on. One such idiom came to public attention in April 2017, when American scientists described what they witnessed the previous year: within a few days, the Kaskawulsh Glacier in the Yukon retreated so much that its meltwater changed direction. Instead of flowing north into the Bering Sea, the water now flows south to the Gulf of Alaska and the Pacific Ocean. To express the magnitude of the change, the scientists used the expression "river piracy."

There's a recently coined insult sometimes aimed at those who seek to take action about climate change, women's rights, LGBTQ rights, and a range of other causes: "snowflake." It's meant to imply weakness, lightness, insignificance. But enough snowflakes falling together can turn into a blizzard.

To Spin a Yarn

Home is an irreplaceable word for everybody who speaks English. We use it in so many expressions and variations that we seldom stop to think about it. From home truths, home pages, home brews and home runs to homelands, homewares and homing pigeons, English hands the concept a leading role in countless expressions and ideas. The language is unusual in its home-loving zeal. French, by contrast, has no single word for home. The meanings French ascribes to *home* are shared out among *maison, résidence, domicile, foyer, appartement, siège, intérieur* and *chez soi*, to name only some. Speakers of French and other languages might find it odd that in English, we're ready to praise an out-of-town or out-of-country destination by calling it a "home away from home."

What kind of home are we talking about, and who should be in charge of it? Those are disputed questions, because the meanings of home—and of the rooms inside it, the clothes that are worn, and the activities carried on there—are all open to debate. English has preserved expressions that are seen today as objectionable by some while being vigorously defended by others. The language describing a home, its contents and its functions can easily become, to use an expression first applied to quarrelling dogs, a bone of contention. Think of the seemingly uncontroversial line "Men make houses, women make homes." Does it honor the abilities of women or does it restrict their freedom? If it gives men financial dominance, does it also banish men from the family's emotional heart?

Idioms that have stood the test of time, as we've seen, are not always innocent. They can be used in political arguments where their useful status as nuggets of proverbial wisdom may hide some unpleasant implications. Consider the proverb "A man's home is his castle." It's the North American version of an older British saying, "An Englishman's home is his castle." Some people believe the line, in either version, celebrates an unjust patriarchal system and can even be used to sanction violence against women and children. Medieval lords held complete authority inside their castles, so why shouldn't men exert all the power in modern homes? *It Matters to Me*, a popular album by the country singer Faith Hill, features a song in which an abusive husband quotes this proverb, insisting it will remain true forever. But to the victimized wife, "His home is his castle and mine is a cage."

More recently, the whistleblower Edward Snowden updated the phrase (while keeping its potentially sexist undertone). In 2016 he observed, "We used to say a man's home is his castle. Today, a man's phone is his castle."

"Charity begins at home" is a proverb that can be traced all the way back to the fourteenth century. When it's taken to mean that each of us has a responsibility to care for those we love, its meaning is benign. But most often it's quoted as a reason to avoid reaching out to help others. "I do believe that charity begins at home," wrote the editor of a West Virginia newspaper in 2015. "And as much as my heart breaks for the Syrian refugees, my gut instinct is to protect my home. Unfortunately, ISIS knows that we are a compassionate, giving nation. And they are and will continue to use that compassion against us." Torn between a gut instinct and a breaking heart, the editor called for US borders to be closed to refugees, and he cited the ancient proverb by way of justification.

It Is Written

"Every kingdom divided against itself is brought to desolation," Jesus observed, "and every city or house divided against itself shall not stand." Less than three years before the outbreak of the US Civil War, the future president Abraham Lincoln quoted the verse in one of the landmark speeches of his career. A few months into Donald Trump's presidency, American commentators of diverse viewpoints were using the line, in tones of grief and anxiety, to characterize their nation. To quote a Huffington Post columnist: "Abraham Lincoln said, 'a house divided against itself cannot stand.' It is difficult for the citizens of America to stand together when our president's primary objective is one of divisiveness." A writer for the political website The Hill added: "No stranger to oft-cited quotes, President Trump might now tweet 'a house divided against itself cannot stand.'"

"A woman's place is in the home"—other constructions say it's in the house or, sometimes, the kitchen. The wording of the idiom varies, but its sentiment remains the same. A character in a play by Aeschylus, the first major dramatist of ancient Greece, says: "Let women stay at home and hold their peace." The English proverb became popular in the nineteenth century, and it's deeply controversial. It has attracted tart rejoinders, notably "A woman's place is in the House of Commons" (or the House of Representatives). Elizabeth Gilbert, in her best-selling book *Committed: A Skeptic Makes Peace with Marriage*, quipped that "a woman's place is in the kitchen . . . sitting in a comfortable chair, with her feet up, drinking a glass of wine and watching her husband cook dinner." Apart from serving as a retort to one familiar proverb, her remark also undercut another: "A woman's work is never done."

In whatever form the idiom may be stated or subverted, "A woman's place is in the home" not only *makes* an editorial judgment: it *is* an editorial judgment.

Legislative buildings around the world are often identified as "houses." Perhaps this is one reason why a significant number of political idioms have a domestic feel about them. During the Second World War, it was the soon-to-be US president, Harry Truman, who coined the line "If you can't stand the heat, get out of the kitchen." In Canada and Britain, a member of Parliament who changes parties is said to "cross the floor." A political leader's team of informal advisers sometimes goes by the name "kitchen cabinet," and this group can overlap with the consultants, money raisers and speechwriters who are collectively known as "back-room boys." If you want to avoid dealing with an issue, you may decide to "sweep it under the carpet" (or the rug). On the other hand, if you're determined to get rid of a problem, you might feel compelled to throw "everything but the kitchen sink" in its direction. A center of political agitation or dissent is often called a "hotbed"—this term originally came from gardening and later became a euphemism for prostitution.

The most evocative of all these idioms is "glass ceiling," a phrase that illustrates the unseen or subtle limits faced by women—or, on occasion, minority groups. A management consultant named Marilyn Loden claims to have invented the expression during a speech she gave in New York in 1978. Loden was talking about the resistance of senior executives to promote women, and she described the existence of an "invisible glass ceiling" to suggest the obstacles that women encounter. The expression took off fast. *The Economist*, for instance, now publishes a country-by-country "glass ceiling index." Related idioms that have, so far, not proved as popular include "glass escalator" (taken by men who speed to the top of traditionally female professions like teaching and nursing) and "sticky floor" (occupied by women who are unlikely to rise in the job market at all).

Of course, not all idioms involving houses and their contents are political. Somebody who "gets out of bed on the wrong side" is behaving in a grumpy and unpleasant manner. Perhaps she's upset at being told to "make her bed and lie in it": admit the consequences of her actions. "Bedroom eyes" are seductive glances, aimed at drawing a potential partner onto what may prove to be a bed of roses but stands an equal chance of becoming a bed of nails. The proverbial bed of roses, shown memorably in the Oscar-winning movie *American Beauty*, is actually a bed of rose petals, without a thorn in sight. A "kitchen sink drama" depicts the lives of ordinary people in a gritty, unsentimental way, and "bargain basement" is a familiar term whose meaning has moved far beyond the lower reaches of department stores. In 2017, for instance, CBC News reported on a land dispute involving indigenous territory in Vancouver; the dispute began way back in 1965, "when residents were able to lease Musqueam land for the bargain basement price of just $400 a year."

Household Names

When you're determined not to fall behind your neighbors in terms of the value of their property, the size of their cars or the prestige of their dinner parties, you're said to be "keeping up with the Joneses." If your neighbors are rich, this can be an arduous task. The expression began life as the title of a *New York World* comic strip, first published in 1913, in which the members of the wealthy Jones family are much talked about but never seen. Just over a century later, *Keeping Up with the Joneses* resurfaced in 2016 as the name of a dismal Hollywood comedy that bombed at the box office.

The idiom also inspired the title of a reality TV series, *Keeping Up with the Kardashians*. The wealthy family members on that show engage in a copious amount of talking and are always seen.

People who maintain their homes in spotless order may see themselves as "house proud." A spokesman for a cleaning technology firm was recently quoted in London's *Daily Mirror* as saying, "Not only does cleaning your home leave you feeling satisfied and house proud, but being able to sit down in a tidy room is often relaxing in itself." Even so, "house proud" is an ambiguous expression. It can imply that someone is too obsessed about the appearance or cleanliness of their property. In a similar vein, the phrase "safe as houses" has a positive meaning: total security. But today it's often used ironically. "Is property really as safe as houses?" asked the historian Niall Ferguson in his book *The Ascent of Money: A Financial History of the World*. "Or is the real estate game more like a house of cards?"

"The apparel oft proclaims the man," Polonius tells his son in Shakespeare's *Hamlet*. Over the centuries the phrase was simplified and modernized into a familiar proverb. Mark Twain quoted and then subverted it when he quipped, "Clothes make the man. Naked people have little or no influence on society." From head to toe, idioms about clothing reflect what we think and feel, not only about the garments in question, but also about the people wearing them.

Let's start at the head. I don't mean to keep these idioms "under my hat"—to keep them quiet, that is. You may decide that some of the expressions are "old hat"—old-fashioned and boring—but knowing one or two of them may prove to be "a feather in your cap," or a symbol of honor. It's not only indigenous North Americans who attached the feathers of eagles and other birds to their headwear; many other cultures have done the same. An English visitor to Hungary wrote in 1599, "It hath been an ancient custom among them that none should wear a feather but he who had killed a Turk"—and for such a killer, "it was lawful to show the number of his slain enemies by the number of feathers in his cap."

"Talking through your hat" began as a description of boasting and turned into an expression for mistake-filled speech, even nonsense. J. K. Rowling can't have had that idiom in mind when she created the Sorting Hat in the Harry Potter books—a hat that has the power to discern a student's inner character. But she may have been recalling the image of a thinking cap. Mind you, it's unlikely that people in the past ever put on a real hat to help them reason. The phrase took over from the earlier "considering cap," a term mentioned by Benjamin Franklin in 1737 when he compiled *The Drinker's Dictionary*, a list of 228 words and idioms for intoxication. The list included gems like "double-tongued," "seen a flock of moons," "drunk as a wheelbarrow," and "Sir Richard has taken off his considering cap."

Certain types of hat, like a stylish fedora, may form part of the repertoire of elegant clothing that's essential for anyone "dressed to the nines." As with other idioms where that number appears—remember "cloud nine"?—the origin of "dressed to the nines" remains obscure. In our time it's more common to dress "smart casual" or "business casual." Many women who adopt this look would have been described, in the past, as "wearing the trousers in the family" (acting as the main decision maker), an idiom that usually conveyed unease and disapproval.

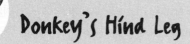 Donkey's Hind Leg

"The days of dressing formally have gone by the board," wrote Carol Dobson of the *Halifax Citizen* in December 2016, "although many do like to don their best bib and tucker." It's rare to come across a recently published sentence that contains a pair of old-fashioned idioms. What exactly did the journalist mean?

Anything "gone by the board" has disappeared or been discarded. This is a naval expression that had the initial sense of an object flung into the sea—think of boards along the sides of a ship. Bibs and tuckers, meanwhile, were decorative pieces of clothing in the eighteenth and nineteenth centuries. Women wore them as items of fashion on the upper body. Young children, then as now, may have been given a bib at mealtime, but they did not wear a tucker: frilly lace above a bodice. Over time, "best bib and tucker" came to mean "best clothes" as sported by men and boys, not only women and girls.

A woman who wants to project an assertive image in the office might wish to master the art of "power dressing." This, or any other style that delivers the right impression, would be what the British call "spot-on," and North Americans "on the button." That idiom derives not from fashion but from the sport of boxing. The button in question was the midpoint of the chin—after a prolonged fight, it often needed sewing up.

Anyone who spends time and money keeping up with the top brand names and the latest trends risks being seen as a "slave to fashion" or a "fashion victim." In July 2017, a style columnist blasted the actress Jennifer Lawrence when she appeared at Haute Couture Fashion Week in Paris wearing an outfit by Christian Dior: "This is the walking definition of 'fashion victim,' in that she's being held hostage by her 'brand ambassador' contract, to the point where we can't even recognize her anymore."

"Fashion victim" is a fairly young term—to express their scorn before the 1990s, people might have turned to the expression "fancy pants." That idiom sounds dated now, although several right-wing websites in the United States deployed it in the headline of an article that appeared in the summer of 2017. It was a sad story about a seventy-nine-year-old professor emeritus of chemistry who forgot to take his dog out of the car on a hot day. By the time he returned to the vehicle, the dog had died. The article said nothing about the man's clothing, but a phrase in the headline— "fancypants college professor"—served as shorthand for "retired professor at expensive university attended mostly by liberals in a state that voted for Hillary Clinton." Few idioms are biased in and of themselves, but any idiom can be used in a biased manner.

"Belt and suspenders" (in North America) and "belt and braces" (in Britain) are idioms expressing caution. If you don't want to risk being left exposed, make doubly sure that your clothes—or your finances—are safe. The need for protection, and the fear of danger, come into play again with the expression "hide behind the skirts." Here, though, a sexist element often creeps in. Look at what the Irish sportswriter Tommy Conlon said about his counterparts from Australia and New Zealand: those reporters "assert their testosterone from a safe space. They hide behind the skirts of their successful teams, be it in cricket or rugby or Australian rules." In the domain of masculine sports, hiding behind skirts counts as an ugly sneer.

Intellectual women were known for a couple of centuries as "bluestockings," after the plain or cheap style of clothing they were purported to favor. Many of the published references to them had a sarcastic tone—the *Edinburgh Review*, for example, complained that "It is disgusting to hear blue-stocking ladies jingle their rhymes." In a more positive vein, a *Vogue* profile of the Italian businesswoman and fashion designer Miuccia Prada suggested that she had chosen to embrace the "book-editor look of yore and taken bluestocking style to silk-stocking heights." The implied message is that it's fine for women to be intelligent as long as they can afford to dress well.

Spoonfuls of sugar

Hush Puppies are a well-known brand of soft suede shoe, and their international success owes a lot to their memorable name and the image of a sad-eyed, long-eared dog. A sales manager named Jim Muir deserves the credit. One day in 1958, on a visit to Tennessee, Muir was served a dish of deep-fried cornmeal balls that went by the name "hush puppies." When he asked his host about the expression, he learned that in the US South, farmers often fed these hush puppies to noisy dogs—supposedly it shut them up. Recalling that an old idiom for sore feet is "barking dogs," Muir saw that "hush puppies" would be a fine way to identify his company's new line of casual footwear.

Think I've gone too far? If so, you might want me to "pull up my socks" (get better at my work) or even "put a sock in it" (shut up). You may choose to see me as a "Goody Two-Shoes"—a reference to a children's book from 1765 in which a one-shoed orphan named Margery Meanwell is nauseatingly grateful when a rich man condescends to give her a new pair. "Goody Two-Shoes" is now an expression that can be applied to anyone who is not only virtuous but smug about it. "If the shoe fits, wear it," you might say. Or you may decide that the author of this book has got "too big for his boots"—more often expressed as "too big for his breeches" back when breeches were a normal piece of clothing.

That's okay. I'm tough as an old boot when it comes to criticism. If you convince me I'm wrong about idioms, I may have to eat my shoes. But only if I end up down at heel—in lasting poverty, that is—may I decide that I picked the wrong profession. I'm here to tell the truth, not spin a yarn.

"Spinning a yarn" has a double meaning, and the two definitions are related. Yarn is any type of fiber—cotton, silk, wool, whatever—that has been prepared for the making of clothes or rope. As a minor character says in Shakespeare's play *All's Well That Ends Well*, "The web of our life is of a mingled yarn, good and ill together." That's a metaphorical use of "yarn," but Shakespeare still had clothing material in mind. A couple of centuries later, the word took a leap and began to mean a long or rambling story. This meaning evolved at sea. While working away at physical yarn—it can be a lengthy and tedious process—sailors would spin a verbal yarn, too.

Historically, clothes making was mainly women's work, and the idioms arising from it are ones that suggest the seriousness and intricacy of the task. "Dyed in the wool" evokes a resolute belief or set of attitudes—though often with a negative tinge. A *Los Angeles Times* review in 2017 of the play *Other Desert Cities* noted that "Polly's alcoholic sister Silda . . . who is staying with them after a stint in rehab, is a dyed-in-the-wool '60s leftie." Behind this expression is an old bit of practical knowledge: wool that is dyed at the earliest stage, before spinning begins, will retain the most enduring colors. The gathering of wool, by contrast, was a job that children could do. In the rural past, they would be sent out to collect tufts of wool, sometimes from bushes and twigs that sheep had brushed against. The task involved much wandering, daydreaming, fantasizing—and so "wool gathering" became an idiom for aimless speculation.

Back to the women. "A stitch in time saves nine" refers to small holes in need of sewing up: the proverb suggests that it's wise to solve problems early instead of waiting until they become serious. If you fail to do this, you'll eventually need to "pick up the threads" and "knit together" whatever is at risk of falling apart, especially if it's "hanging by a thread." Perhaps you'll have to "mend your ways" in the process. These idioms, as you'll have noticed, all deal with fixing or preserving the quality of things. They are, you might say, tightly woven into the fabric of language. Jeanne Calment, a Frenchwoman who lived to be 122 years old, once apologized for her great age by saying: "Excuse me if I'm clinging on to life. But my parents wove from tight thread." Madame Calment maintained her lucidity to the end—unlike so many people, she never "lost the thread."

Donkey's Hind Leg

"*The Birdwatcher* Reveals Distaff Side of Industry at Vancouver International Women in Film Festival," ran a headline in the *Georgia Straight* newspaper in 2016. "The distaff side" is an ostentatious way of referring to women. But even people who understand the meaning of the idiom seldom have a clear sense of what a distaff is, or was.

It's a staff about a meter long, usually held under the left arm, around which wool or flax could be wound so as to keep it free of tangles. As an instrument of spinning, the distaff became a prototype for women's work—and ultimately for the female members of a family. "The Crown of France never falls to the distaff," declared an English book published in 1706. The male counterpart to the distaff side—not that you're likely to find it in any headline—is "the spear side."

Threads and yarn must be woven into cloth, and there's an old expression from weaving that evokes the whole structure of something: "warp and woof." It has nothing to do with distortions or dogs. Here the warp refers to the lengthwise threads in a loom, and the woof consists of the cross strands. Together they make up an entire substance that can't easily be pulled apart. In May 2017, faced with the imponderability of *Twin Peaks: The Return*, a puzzled reviewer for *Slant* asked: "How important is this particular thread to the overall warp and woof of the tapestry that David Lynch and Mark Frost are weaving?"

He wouldn't have an answer until the series was all sewn up.

Clothes are made, clothes are worn, clothes get dirty. Dirt can be a useful metaphor not only for obvious transgressions like crime, illicit sex and vicious politics, but also for unacceptable feelings. It's no surprise, in that light, to find that idioms involving washing and cleaning often reflect the sheer strength of dirt.

Although it sounds deceptively mild, one of the most powerful expressions is "air your dirty laundry in public." (Sometimes "linen" replaces "laundry.") There's even a popular website named celebdirtylaundry.com. But it's not only the rich and famous who are scared of exposure. A 2017 article in the Asian American magazine *Hyphen* quoted a first-time mother: "We don't talk about being pregnant and giving birth . . . In Korean society, you don't air your dirty laundry. Within the nuclear family, you keep your stuff very private." Dirty laundry, in this instance, refers to fear and depression, emotions that bring shame because they are unacceptable in the woman's community.

Only a small number of people may see or hear about the dirty laundry in question, yet its impact can still be intense. With "mudslinging," by contrast, the goal is public humiliation. It's an activity designed to cause pain. If someone has "dished the dirt" on you, you may be in disgrace—your reputation has been "dragged through the mud." Some, maybe even all, of those insults and attacks were without foundation. But, to quote a sardonic proverb, "If you throw enough mud at the wall, some of it will stick." Mudslinging is the modern extension of a venerable idiom, "throw dirt," as used by an overheated English writer named James Howell in 1647: "Any sterquilinious rascal is licensed to throw dirt in the faces of sovereign princes in open printed language." *Sterquilinious* means belonging to a dunghill.

Flash forward three hundred years. Shortly after the US Air Force dropped atomic bombs on the Japanese cities of Hiroshima and Nagasaki, the visionary scientist behind the weapons' development, J. Robert Oppenheimer, experienced deep remorse. "I feel we have blood on our hands," he told Harry Truman, the president who had given the go-ahead for the attack. Truman declined to express guilt. "Never mind," he said to Oppenheimer, "it'll all come out in the wash." Sometimes this expression suggests "Everything will be revealed in the end," but Truman was using it to mean "Things will work out just fine." Presumably he felt, unlike Oppenheimer, that any lingering pain would soon be washed away. "It will all come out in the wash" is an upbeat rejoinder to the downbeat expression "It won't wash"—meaning "It won't be believed" or "It won't stand up to scrutiny."

When you wash your hands of someone, you refuse to have anything more to do with him. You leave him hung out to dry: he's not your responsibility. You may believe he's all washed up. Idioms like these are strikingly terse and cold. In the political sphere, we still use the dated expression "laundry list" to refer to a long set of demands, many of which can't reasonably be met, and the newer idiom "money laundering" for an activity that is dirty by its very nature. Even the verb phrase "clean up" has mixed meanings. It can be a necessary thing to do ("Volunteers cleaned up 400 pounds of garbage and other pollutants from the beaches and waterways of Encinitas"), but it can also be used in a more aggressive sense ("*Mad Max* cleaned up at the Oscars, just as it should have").

The duality of feeling in all this was summed up when Jim Watson, the mayor of Ottawa, gave a "state of the city" speech that minimized the challenges facing his community. "If you're going to read a laundry list," a CBC reporter dryly suggested, "the dirty laundry should be on it, too."

"Better the devil you know": apart from being the name of a song by Kylie Minogue, this expression suggests a serious mistrust of change. Perhaps there's an inherent conservatism in the very nature of idioms—a suspicion that change is likely to be for the worse. That feeling shows through in how English expressions treat the transformation of raw food. You'd think these would be idioms of pure delight—who doesn't enjoy a home-cooked meal? But if so, you'd be wrong.

"What's cooking?" is a vivid way of asking "What's going on?" It doesn't show any confidence that the food emerging from the kitchen will be all that we hope. True, that steak may be "done to a T." But it might also be "burnt to a crisp." And if you got your fingers burned in the process, you're probably unwilling to take the risk again. Or perhaps you don't have the time, as you're the "chief cook and bottlewasher" around here. In other words, you have too much to do, some of it important, much of it not.

"Tommy and an ever-growing band of would-be escapees . . . find themselves going from one frying pan to another fire": that line comes from an online review of Christopher Nolan's 2017 movie *Dunkirk*. "Out of the frying pan, into the fire" is a time-honored way to suggest that things are getting worse—if you tried to make things better, you failed. Speaking of failure, "your goose is cooked" when your plans have been wrecked. A *Politico* report on the Republican effort to pass a new health-care bill in the United States quoted a "senior West Wing aide" as saying, "The goose was cooked with the first House bill." The politicians were left to "stew in their own juice"—endure their bitterness and frustration. They might as well have "roasted snow in a furnace," for the task was a futile one.

Combing the Giraffe

When we turn away from a particular task and move on to something else, we may say, "I've got bigger fish to fry." (Sometimes "better" or "other" replaces "bigger.") In French and Dutch, you don't pick up a frying pan at a moment like this. Instead, you look around for a stray cat. In 2013, when a star player on France's national soccer team declined to sing the country's anthem, the team manager said: "What right do I have to make him sing 'La Marseillaise'? We have other cats to whip."

The Finnish language doesn't torture cats. But don't stray far from the kitchen. If a Finn has what we call "a bone to pick," she'll say, "I have a hen to pluck with you."

In response we can always attempt to "brew something up"—and the result may be a terrific batch of beer. But more likely, "trouble is brewing." Perhaps that's because someone has planted false information, thereby "cooking the books" (or the accounts). Or maybe it's because what's bubbling away in the cauldron turns out to be a witches' brew.

"Too many cooks spoil the broth"—along with a less common variant, "too many cooks in the kitchen"—suggests that quality suffers when several people do the same job. If you feel uncertain whether to obey this advice or accept a proverb that says precisely the opposite ("Many hands make light work"), be careful not to "fall between two stools." There are times when two options can't be reconciled, and to combine them would result in failure.

Or, if you're feeling mischievous, you can blend a couple of well-known proverbs and thereby create a "perverb." The American writer and poet Harry Mathews invented this word in 1977. Two of his perverbs were "The road to Hell wasn't paved in a day" and "Bird in the hand, sailor's delight." Go ahead and try it for yourself.

English doesn't enforce grammatical distinctions between male and female in the way that French, Spanish, German, and many other languages do. We don't arbitrarily decide that a table is female and a bed is male. But in the realm of words and idioms, English makes it very clear that one sex has long been dominant over the other. A man can be a playboy; a woman is a slut. A man would "sow his wild oats;" a woman was a "brazen hussy." The conquests made by a "lady killer"—or a Don Juan—might include a "fallen woman," a "loose woman," a "scarlet woman" and a "kept woman." By contrast, the female equivalent of Don Juan is not "Doña Juanita" but a nymphomaniac.

The language of hip-hop is full of derogatory words about women: *Ho. Shorty* (or shawty). *Breezie. Milkshake. Chickenhead. Dime.* This last is especially interesting because it emerges from the same 1 to 10 rating system for women's bodies that Donald Trump notoriously used—10 (a dime) being the highest. Rappers deploy *dime* as an ostensible term of praise, but the word may also suggest that to a man, even the most attractive woman is worth ten cents. Were things so different in the past? In the slang of eighteenth-century London, "laced mutton" referred to a prostitute, "buttock and tongue" meant a scolding wife, and "tenant for life" was a married man.

When the young Elvis Presley was being interviewed one day, he was asked: "Why aren't you married?" Presley replied with a question of his own: "Why buy the cow when you can get the milk for free?" The meaning of this old expression used to be financial, but over the centuries, it became almost exclusively sexual. To this day, some parents still quote it to their daughters. There is, I'm happy to say, a rejoinder:

"Why buy the pig when all you want is a little sausage?"

Dark Horse

The most valuable teams in professional sports belong to the National Football League. Major League Baseball comes in second, and the National Basketball Association third. The Premier League of British soccer ranks fourth, although if you add together the value of all the teams in Europe's soccer leagues, they would outrank even the NFL. The National Hockey League, in case you were wondering, is a distant fifth. That's a measure of the financial status of major sports in the early twenty-first century. But it's a far cry from what you might call their linguistic status, as measured by their impact on the English language and by the number of expressions that began life in each sport.

Successful idioms hang around for centuries. They have a richness of meaning that transcends their source and is available to everyone: women and men, rich and poor, old and young. That's not the case for specialized sporting phrases like "dead-ball rebound," "five-hole" and "backcourt violation." Those expressions mean a lot to fans of the game in question, but they leave everybody else clueless. Basketball and hockey are relatively young sports, and they've contributed little to the mainstream of the English language. Ask me about them again in a hundred years.

Sports have been defined as a moral replacement for war. In ancient Greece, warring city-states would stop fighting for the duration of the Olympic Games. The end of the games, of course, saw a prompt resumption of conflict. The first Olympics included horse races, footraces, jumping, throwing, boxing and wrestling. Not all aspects of the original games were revived in the late nineteenth century when the modern Olympics took shape—we no longer sacrifice a herd of oxen to Zeus, for example. But many of the Greek competitions have gone on to exert an influence on the English language, and none more so than boxing.

Whenever you say "throw in the towel" (give up), "on the ropes" (the verge of defeat) or "below the belt" (unfair), you're using an expression that began life in the ring. Admittedly, the boxing idioms we use today did not grow from the jasmine-scented pastures of Mount Olympus. Most of them were born in the smoky dives of nineteenth-century England and America. The rules of the sport were named after the Marquess of

Queensberry, who endorsed them in 1867, but boxing was never just an aristocratic pursuit—it was a sport for the common people. And the common people immortalized it in words.

"Roll with the punches": learn how to adapt. "In your corner": willing to lend help and support. "Blow-by-blow account": a detailed description, omitting nothing. "Knockout punch": a blow that ends any sort of combat. The list goes on. Boxing is a fight, pure and simple, and the human urge (the male urge, in particular) to imagine life as a fight has led to the adoption of boxing idioms in many other realms.

When a boxer is "down and out," for instance, he's been knocked unconscious and is unable to get up. At the beginning of the twentieth century, the expression migrated to the slums, referring to people so destitute they were unable to look after themselves. The first book by the great British author George Orwell was a memoir entitled *Down and Out in Paris and London*. A dizzy, much-pummeled boxer is, we would say today, concussed; earlier phrases for that condition were "punch-drunk" and "slaphappy." Both expressions have taken on a new life outside the sport. *Punch-Drunk Love* was the name of an Adam Sandler comedy about an emotionally bruised couple struggling to connect. And "slaphappy" has come to mean any state of casual fun or irresponsibility—in 2017, travel writer Rick Steves described Oktoberfest in Munich as "a slaphappy world of sausages, fancy hats and maidens with flowers in their hair." (Not forgetting a million gallons of beer, of course.)

Combing the Giraffe

Bullfighting is, as you might expect, a vital resource for Spanish expressions. One of them, "See the bulls from the barrier," alludes to the ability of a fighter to leap out of the ring when a bull is on his heels. In English we might say "Look on from the sidelines." The nature of language seems to require that, as a rule, idioms are best translated by other idioms: straightforward literal translations fall far short. The Spanish expression "consider the bull" is very similar in meaning to "test the water" or "put out feelers," while "catch the bull," oddly enough, is roughly equivalent to "run out of time."

Then there's the curious Spanish phrase "Until the tail, it's all bull." It has received a variety of English translations, ranging from "It ain't over till the fat lady sings" to "While there's life, there's hope." Perhaps the closest English equivalent, though, is "Don't count your chickens until they're hatched." A matador must be prepared for surprises: victory over even a wounded bull can't be taken for granted.

Boxing is not the only sport from the ancient Olympics to have generated a range of English idioms. Thanks to wrestling, we have the phrase "no holds barred" (a graphic way of saying "anything goes"). Thanks to hurdling and high jumping, we have "low bar" and "high bar" (standards that must be met). Thanks to horse racing, we have a host of expressions: "home stretch," "down to the wire," "in the running," "dead heat," and more.

Many of those phrases are common in political discourse, as if elections were horse races and candidates were either the jockeys or the animals they ride. The competitive impulse that drives many people to enter politics—to "throw their hat into the ring," as a boxing idiom puts it—also drives how politics is reported and spoken about. A candidate may be "jockeying for position." To alter the metaphor, she needs to be clever if she's to win the race, particularly if she's "a dark horse."

The dark horse is among the most intriguing idioms to emerge from horse racing. It has nothing to do with the color of the animal's skin. On the contrary, it goes back to the original meaning of "in the dark," referring not to a lack of knowledge but to secrecy or concealment. In 1831, the young English author—and future prime minister—Benjamin Disraeli adapted that sense of "dark" for the racetrack in his novel *The Young Duke*, when he wrote: "A dark horse, which had never been thought of . . . rushed past the grand stand in sweeping triumph." Its victory was entirely unexpected, making it a "dark" horse. Before long, the phrase was being applied to political figures who hoped to step out of the shadows and take power. As any politician or athlete knows, it's one thing to run the race, but quite another to win it.

And with any race, including the political kind, there's always a risk of betting on the wrong horse.

Two sports that were born in Scotland centuries ago are curling and golf. Curling is at least five hundred years old, but its expressions have failed to spread outward from the ice rink into the rest of the language—the rocks in "get your rocks off" are not curling stones. Golf is another matter. Unlike curling, it became a popular activity in the United States and England, and some elements of its lexicon are now familiar even to people who loathe the game.

A "hole in one," for instance, can refer to anything done with perfection, especially on the first time of trying. (Has there ever been a droller newspaper headline than "Grandmother of Eight Makes Hole in One"?) Like "hole in one," the expression "make the cut" has a technical meaning: to score well enough over the first two days of a four-day tournament that the golfer meets the cutoff point and is allowed to play the two final rounds. More widely, it means to meet some required level. In 2015, the Science Alert website published a story with the headline "New Criteria for What Makes a Planet Means Pluto Still Doesn't Make the Cut." Poor Pluto: it's now officially an "ice dwarf."

"Bunker" is a name for the sand traps that have been the ruin of many a round of golf. These traps generally lie below the surrounding grass. In the Second World War, the word was used to evoke an underground shelter, and from there it evolved to mean any kind of shelter or fortified building. As CBC News reported in 2010, "Two Quebec cities say the Hells Angels have outstanding property tax bills on their vacant bunkers." In modern warfare, a "bunker buster" is a weapon powerful enough to destroy the protective shelters of enemy fighters, and, more generally, the phrase "bunker mentality" refers to organizations or people who feel constantly under attack.

Spoonfuls of sugar

A golfing hole that a competent player could be expected to complete in four strokes is called a "par four"; longer holes are "par fives," shorter ones "par threes." Anything that happens in a predictable manner is said to be "par for the course" and anything good enough to escape complaint is "up to par"—there's nothing unusual about either of those idioms. But confusion arises with the expressions "below par" and "above par."

Golfers hope to finish each round below par. The higher their score rises above par, the worse their day becomes. The golfing meaning, in short, is the exact opposite of the everyday meaning, where "below par" refers to a substandard performance and "above par" an excellent one. Blame the multiple senses of "par" for the mix-up. Originally, "par" denoted the value of a currency or the face value of a security. Used in a general context, "above par" and "below par" go back to the word's older meaning, not to the golf course.

The entertaining vocabulary of golf—"double bogey," "improved lie," "postage stamp green" and so on—pales beside the picturesque, even peculiar lexicon of cricket. It's one of the most popular sports in the former British Empire—except for Canada, that is. The vocabulary of cricket includes memorable expressions like "maiden over," "sticky wicket," "silly mid off" and "donkey drop." Many cricket idioms that are familiar in British

English ("gone for a duck," for instance, meaning a batsman's score of zero) are unknown in North America. But some have crossed over successfully into the international language.

A "hat trick," for instance, is a common expression to indicate three goals scored by the same player in a game of soccer or hockey. It can be used in nonsporting circles, too: witness a headline in *The Economist*—"Erdoğan's hat trick"—after Turkey's prime minister won his third election in a row. But originally, a hat trick was a rare achievement on the cricket pitch. It meant a bowler who removed three batsmen with consecutive balls—in the nineteenth century, a bowler's team would reward such an accomplishment by giving him a new hat. To do something "off your own bat" is to do it yourself, with no outside request or command; this too began as a cricketing expression. As for "daisy cutter"—the name for an immense bomb—the credit (or should it be blame?) is often given to cricket, where the expression refers to a ball that rolls along the pitch or bounces more than once before reaching the batsman. But "daisy cutter" can also be used in horse racing and baseball.

Have you been "champing at the bit" (a horse-racing idiom) for me to finally get round to baseball? Were you worried I could "go the distance" (a boxing expression) without facing up to the language from the diamond? Did you want me to "jump the gun" (this phrase comes from track and field) and deal with baseball before everything else?

Relax. The time has come.

How many idioms started off in the game of baseball? It's hard to give even a "ballpark figure." But beyond a doubt, baseball has had more influence on the language of North America than any other team sport. As the Washington sportswriter Thomas Boswell once wrote, "Conversation is the blood of baseball. It flows through the game, an invigorating system of anecdotes. Ballplayers are tale tellers who have polished their malarkey and winnowed their wisdom for years." Small wonder that so many baseball expressions have flowed into the great river of American speech.

Not that baseball is entirely an American sport. Something very like it had been played in England for decades long before it became America's national pastime—indeed, the game is mentioned in Jane Austen's novel *Northanger Abbey*, written in about 1803. The teenage heroine, Catherine Morland, is described as preferring "cricket, base ball, riding on horseback, and running about the country . . . to books—or at least books of information." The widespread belief that Abner Doubleday invented baseball in 1839 in Cooperstown, New York, proves only that fake news and alternative facts were prevalent in the United States long before the advent of Twitter and Breitbart.

During the late nineteenth and early twentieth century, tens of millions of immigrants poured into New York and other American ports. They didn't learn the idioms of football or basketball, at least not immediately; instead they learned the language of baseball. It was inescapable. Perhaps they felt that American English, with all its complexities and inconsistencies, often threw them a "curve ball"; but they persevered. Anyone who didn't master English was likely to be "caught off base," even to the point of "striking out" in the new country. Yet most of the newcomers "stepped up to the plate." Some American practices and beliefs came at them "out of left field." Maybe they didn't succeed "right off the bat." But in the end, they were "home free."

Household Names

In 1919, the favorites to win the World Series were the Chicago White Sox, led by one of the best outfielders in the game, Shoeless Joe Jackson. (He earned his nickname as a teenager when blisters on his feet hurt so much that one day he took off his shoes before stepping up to bat.) The White Sox faced the Cincinnati Reds in a best-of-nine series, and they lost five games to three. Months later, news leaked out that some Chicago players had accepted $5,000 each from gamblers to throw the series. The team went down in infamy as the "Black Sox."

Was Shoeless Joe Jackson part of the conspiracy? He was a barely literate millworker from a small town in South Carolina, and although, at one point, he confessed to being in on the fix, his play during the World Series had been superb. Later he denied all involvement. After he was indicted by a grand jury, the *Chicago Daily News* ran an article under the headline "Say It Ain't So, Joe." The line soon became a catchphrase, available to anyone who wants to express ironic regret. When a politician has that particular first name, the temptation to use the expression is often too great for reporters and headline writers to resist. But there was no particular Joseph in sight in May 2017 when a columnist for the *Albany Times Union* wrote: "Racist fans in Boston? Say it ain't so, Joe."

Sometimes an idiom changes its meaning to such an extreme degree that the disparity between the original sense and the later one is dramatic. Take the baseball expression "hit-and-run." On the diamond, it's a set play in which a baserunner takes off early, hoping the batter will make contact with the ball; if he doesn't, the baserunner may well be thrown out. Whether or not the runner succeeds, it's a deliberate strategy. The expression was in widespread use in the late nineteenth century when the first cars appeared on North American roads. And by 1924, "hit-and-run" had taken on a much crueler sense, describing a driver who fails to stop after an accident. Both uses of the phrase survive to this day, although the implications of the hitting and the running could hardly be more different.

More commonly, a sports expression will be stretched into a wider meaning without losing all its previous connotations. A switch-hitter, on the baseball diamond, is someone who can bat either left-handed or right-handed. Today, in bars and clubs, "switch-hitter" is slang for a bisexual person who will sleep with either men or women. "Screwball" is a baseball term for a pitch, thrown especially by left-handers, that uses a reverse spin going against the ball's natural curve. The word emerged in the 1920s, and within a few years it was being used in a metaphorical sense to mean an eccentric, a lunatic or a fool. Rollicking Hollywood films of the era were promptly called screwball comedies. In just a decade, "screwball" had moved from being a new type of baseball pitch to a person to a movie. Idioms can evolve fast, but seldom as fast as this.

Tomatoes on Your Eyes

The New York Yankees had a catcher in the 1950s and 1960s, Lorenzo Pietro "Yogi" Berra, who became better known for his misuse of the English language than for his formidable baseball skills. He's known for a number of famous utterances: "Pair up in threes." "We made too many wrong mistakes." "It gets late early out there" (he was describing the afternoon light in Yankee Stadium). "If you can't imitate him, don't copy him." "I looked like this when I was young, and I still do." And my favorite: "Always go to other people's funerals. Otherwise they won't go to yours."

On the other hand, he did not say "It's hard to make predictions, especially about the future." That sentiment was apparently first given voice by a Danish politician in the 1930s and translated into English a generation later. It has since been ascribed to Yogi Berra, Nostradamus, Mark Twain, Niels Bohr, Samuel Goldwyn and doubtless many other people too. Every time you come across the line, feel free to quote another comment often attributed to Berra: "It's déjà vu all over again."

Yogi Berra was among the many baseball stars who plied their trade at Yankee Stadium in New York's northernmost borough, the Bronx. I always assumed that the expression "Bronx cheer"—a contemptuous noise, the same as what the English call "blowing a raspberry"—derived from the team's notoriously demanding fans, an idea that has often been proposed in print and online. But there's a problem with it. Yankee Stadium opened in 1923. Before that point, the team played in the northern reaches of the island of Manhattan. And the novelist Damon Runyon had already used the phrase "jolly old Bronx cheer" in a newspaper piece about a college football game in 1921. Clearly the uninhibited residents of the Bronx knew how to make their feelings heard before the Yankees moved there.

Driven by the growing power of radio and by the gin-soaked imagination of writers like Runyon, baseball conferred on its leading stars some of the wildest nicknames of any sport. It's rare today for athletes to have nicknames as memorable as ones belonging to Hall of Fame players from the first half of the twentieth century: the Georgia Peach (Ty Cobb), the Yankee Clipper (Joe DiMaggio), Little Napoleon (John McGraw), the Mahatma (Branch Rickey), the Sultan of Swat (Babe Ruth), the Flying Dutchman (Honus Wagner), and Big Poison (Paul Waner).

So much for baseball idioms. I haven't touched all the bases, I realize. But I intend to play hardball and go to bat now for some other sports.

•   •   •

"The beautiful game" is a common nickname for soccer, or "football" as it's usually known in Britain and Ireland. Pelé, a great Brazilian soccer player in the 1950s, made the expression widely known—the dedication to his autobiography reads, "I dedicate this book to all the people who have made this great game the Beautiful Game."

One of the least beautiful experiences for any soccer player is to score an "own goal"—to put the ball into one's own net by mistake, while defending against the other team. The expression has wider resonance. In May 2017, for instance, the Archbishop of Canterbury paid a delicate diplomatic visit to Israel and Palestine, in the course of which he played in a soccer match with local children of several religions. "Justin Welby Avoids Own Goal in Trip to Holy Land": that was how the *Guardian* headlined its report.

Many sports enjoy an overlapping vocabulary, and it can be hard to know which one lies at the source of a given phrase. "Kickoff" is a British expression that migrated into American football, but it's unclear whether it began on the soccer pitch or the rugby field. The idiom is widely used now in politics, too, as in "kick off the election campaign." On the other hand, some expressions sound as if they should be sports idioms, even when they have no connection to sports: "kicking an idea around," for example, is an American outgrowth of "kick around," meaning to wander aimlessly. "Moving the goalposts" is an odd example of a sporting phrase that was metaphorical right from the start. It was born in Britain, and the earliest-known example came from the *Scotsman* newspaper in 1924. The context was political: "The Liberals, having been beaten, not only wanted to change the rules of the game, but wanted to shift the goal posts because they could not play any more."

Compared to baseball, American football has given relatively few idioms to the broader language. An "end run" is a football play in which the ball carrier rushes around the end of the offensive line instead of charging straight ahead. Off the field, it can evoke any evasive tactic or avoidance ploy. The phrase has obvious relevance in the world of politics, as does "playbook." Originally, a playbook meant a written collection of moves each football player had to master. But just before Canada's federal election in 2015, *Chatelaine* invited readers "inside Justin Trudeau's home, family life and political playbook." The lofty rhetoric of political speeches is regularly at odds with the down-to-earth metaphors that journalists use to describe the people making those speeches.

Spoonfuls of sugar

If you're in search of bewildering expressions, look no further than "the whole nine yards." It's an Americanism, and most people assume it refers to the methodical progress of a football team down the field. But to obtain a first down, you have to move the ball ten yards, not nine, and nobody says "the whole ten yards." Suggestions about the phrase's origin have involved everything from the length of a hangman's noose to the size of a rich man's grave. Some people have claimed it's military slang from either the Vietnam War or the Second World War.

That can't be right, because the concept behind the phrase goes back to at least 1912, when a newspaper in rural Kentucky declared, "As we have been gone for a few days and failed to get all the news for this issue, we will give you the whole six yards in our next." The whole *six* yards? As other examples show—think of "cloud eight" turning into "cloud nine"—idioms have a habit of mysteriously growing over time.

Canadian politics is one of the few spheres of language where hockey has made a lasting impression. After the British Columbia election of May 2017 left the Green Party in a position of both new influence and high vulnerability, Global News ran a story with the headline "Greens Face Stickhandling Act, Experts Say." A year earlier, when Doug Clovechok was selected as the BC Liberal candidate in Columbia River-Revelstoke, he said, "I'm not afraid to drop the gloves if there's an issue that needs the gloves to be dropped." Clovechok's pugnacity may have helped him win the seat.

"Stickhandle" and "drop the gloves" have dipsy-doodled beyond the hockey arena into the public realm. Typically, idioms move from the arena, the stadium, the course or the ring into general discourse. But occasionally they shift in the opposite direction. Ever since the Canadian Pacific Railway was completed in 1885, "coast to coast" has been an idiom that proudly

evokes the nation's size and aspirations—more recently, thanks
to a heightened awareness of the Arctic, "coast to coast to coast"
has supplanted it. But in hockey parlance, "coast to coast" now
describes a skater who picks up the puck behind his or her own
goal line and carries it all the way into the other team's end. At
the micro level of language as well as the macro level of Olympic
sport, patriotism and hockey can be hard to separate.

So far, the sports I've been talking about all began as male pur-
suits. Their heroes are surrogate warriors. Of course, millions of
women take part in soccer, hockey, basketball and other sports,
but the dominant context continues to be a male one. In only a
few sports have women been as prominent as men—figure skating and gymnastics come to mind—and the specific vocabulary
of those sports has remained a largely private matter. The only
Olympic sports restricted to women are rhythmic gymnastics
and synchronized swimming; again, neither has provided any idioms to the wider language. The most important jumps in figure
skating are an Axel, a Lutz and a Salchow. Not many outsiders
could explain the differences between those jumps, and none of
them has become part of an idiom with any meaning beyond the
ice rink. More tellingly, all of them are named after male skaters.

In saying all this, I may be "skating on thin ice"—taking a certain risk, that is. "Get your skates on!" is a British idiom meaning
"Hurry up!" But those two expressions emerged from skating
as a simple activity, not a competitive sport. That's also true for
idioms involving swimming and diving, a pair of Olympic sports

that belong to women just as much as men. The English expressions born in the water, so to speak, are not about competition. They're about survival skills, or the lack of them.

"Sink or swim," we might say to people if we have no intention of helping them out. Perhaps they're happy to just dive in. But if they're thrown in at the deep end, there's no chance for them to begin by getting their feet wet (learning gradually)—they have to face a challenge right away. They may be out of their depth, in which case it will be tough for them to keep their heads above water. The difficulty is all the greater if they're swimming against the tide, or the current, or the stream—English offers a novice swimmer all three options. What concerned our forebears, on the evidence of their language choices, were not the pleasures of watery exercise but the dangers of watery death.

Donkey's Hind Leg

"Swimming pool" is one of those compound nouns we use so naturally, we seldom stop to think about it. It wasn't always how people identified the place they would go to swim. "Swimming bath" used to be the preferred expression. The doomed ship *Titanic*, for example, had a "swimming bath" on its F-deck. When Winston Churchill traveled across Canada in 1929, he spent a night at Radium Hot Springs in British Columbia. Describing the experience to his wife back in England, he wrote: "We bathed night and morning in the open air

Some expressions about water, such as "ride the crest of a wave," do seem more upbeat in meaning. This idiom refers to a person or movement that's becoming ever more popular. A politician, a singer, a fashion trend, a belief system—any of them can ride a wave's crest. But be careful. As surfers know, every wave ultimately breaks. Even a positive phrase about the power of water holds a subsurface warning: popularity won't last for long.

Games that involve an agility of mind, not body, have also left their mark on English. Think about chess for a moment. When you're forced to obey orders, you're "a pawn in the system," and if you run out of options, you're said to be "checkmated." The final moves in a match, when most of the pieces are off the board, are called the endgame. The Irish writer Samuel Beckett made this idiom the title of one of his most intense and agonizing plays. *Endgame* is sometimes used today to evoke the final stages of a battle. A more recent expression is "back to square one"—to begin again, something chess never allows a player to do. The origin of this idiom is most likely the childhood game of Snakes and Ladders.

Surprisingly, chess—despite its great age—has contributed far fewer expressions to the English language than have games of cards. You may not even realize that a few of these idioms were born around the card table. A "grand slam," for example, has one meaning in baseball (a home run with the bases loaded), and another in tennis and golf (victory in the year's four major tournaments). But it originated in the game of bridge, where it means winning all the tricks. Suppose I boast about winning a grand slam even though I haven't done so. If you challenge me, you've "called my bluff"—an idiom that derives from poker, where a gifted player can sometimes win a lot of money by guile and nerve.

Spoonfuls of sugar

You can be sure it's not a computer chip that people carry on their shoulders—but is it a potato chip, a poker chip, a chocolate chip or what? Actually it's a wood chip, and one of considerable size. "Chip on his shoulder" is an American idiom that once conveyed a literal meaning. As a Long Island newspaper noted in 1830, "When two churlish boys were determined to fight, a chip would be placed on the shoulder of one, and the other demanded to knock it off."

So the idiom began with a brawl. Poker chips, by contrast, are the ones referred to in the expression "when the chips are down"—that is, when times are tough and a decision has to be made. "Cash in your chips" also comes from poker: it's what you do when the game is over. It's also American slang for "die."

In any field, it's risky to keep on bluffing. If you do it for too long, other people will see what you're up to. Then they'll realize your success has been built on a "house of cards" that can tumble down at any moment—look no further than the TV series *House of Cards*, about a cutthroat politician.

You can't win all the tricks if you've been dealt a bad hand. Maybe the deck was stacked against you. But perhaps you've got an ace up your sleeve? Or is there a wild card that can bring you success? In that event, you'll "come up trumps" or "turn up trumps"—a very old expression, first spoken by a cardplayer in the sixteenth century. The urge to vanquish opponents was as strong then as it is now.

Which makes it all the more surprising, perhaps, that the expression "a good sport" refers to somebody who copes well with embarrassment or defeat.

Loose Lips Sink Ships

At-*ten*-tion!

War provides the starting gun for many idioms that went on to become popular in times of peace. We may not realize it, but every time we talk about flying colors or basket cases, nose diving or being unflappable, we're using language that had a military birth.

Some of these idioms go back centuries. For example, you often hear of politicians abruptly altering their policy on a crucial issue, a reversal commonly called an about-face. The expression comes from the Napoleonic Wars of the early nineteenth century, when, in the vocabulary of the British army, an "about-face" was a command in a military drill. An about-face is very similar to an about-turn, which also began as a drill command. Idioms have the power to freeze language in its tracks, and both "about-face" and "about-turn" have preserved an old, discarded meaning of "about": a swivel or a rotation.

Beating a retreat—sometimes written or spoken with an adjective added for extra flavor, as in "beating a hasty retreat"—emerged from a slightly earlier period. In the late seventeenth and eighteenth centuries, when soldiers were told to disengage from battle or simply stop fighting for the night, the order would reach them by the signal of a drumbeat. The beat, often played by a "little drummer boy," would keep the men in step as they withdrew. Evidently the drum took over a role once performed by the bagpipes and the trumpet, because in the Middle Ages and the Renaissance those instruments were the ones that would "sound the retreat" for soldiers. Today, we're more likely to speak of a cabinet minister beating a hasty retreat after pulling an about-face.

We use the phrase "rank and file" to mean the ordinary members of any group. "Ohio CEOs Paid 290 Times More Than Average Rank-and-File Worker," ran a headline in an Ohio newspaper in May 2017. But the expression used to refer to the formations of rows and columns in which soldiers were drawn up for drill. (It's when they were marching in rank and file that they'd be instructed to make an about-turn.) The night before a battle, officers might steal a march on the enemy by secretly changing the position of their troops. Now "steal a march" can refer to any advantage gained by acting in advance of the competition. On the actual battlefield, stealing a march has been replaced by launching a preemptive strike.

It Is Written

I live by the sword and die by the sword, the hip-hop artist Lil Wayne raps in his 2013 song "God Bless Amerika." The image is a common one and, whether or not Lil Wayne knew it, it goes back to the Bible. Jesus reproved a follower by saying: "Put your sword back into its place, for all those who take the sword will die by the sword." Yet the image's original source was not the New Testament but *Agamemnon*, a tragedy by the Greek dramatist Aeschylus, which was performed in Athens in 458 BC. "By the sword you did your work," one of its characters laments, "and by the sword you die." Some elements of ancient Greek thought had a significant impact on the New Testament, which was originally written in Greek.

Another idiom with a complex history is "bite the dust," meaning to die. In Homer's *Iliad*, Agamemnon prays that Hector's comrades will "bite the dust as they fall dying round him." Or to be exact, that's what Agamemnon prays in a nineteenth-century English translation of the *Iliad*. The translator, Samuel Butler, almost certainly had a verse from the Psalms in mind: "They that dwell in the wilderness shall bow before him, and his enemies shall lick the dust." Butler changed licking to biting, with lasting results for the language. Here again, English drew on the twin influences of the Bible and ancient Greece.

Students and managers, writers and researchers, scientists and politicians: we all face deadlines. When a due date is approaching too fast, we complain about the unfair deadline—although without one, we might never finish the job. "Deadline" is a terse figure of speech with a military origin. It arose during the US Civil War, when it had the most literal of meanings. Both the Confederate and the Union armies are said to have operated prisons with dead lines, which were drawn inside the wall or stockade of a military prison. Any prisoner who stepped beyond the line in an attempt to reach the wall would be shot. Fortunately, the penalty for missing a deadline now is a little milder.

Another expression from American warfare that has slipped into common parlance is "bury the hatchet." A conflict having ended, the chiefs or leading warriors of indigenous nations would bury their tomahawks at a sacred location as a sign of lasting peace. The image soon made its way into English. The Treaty of Hopewell, signed in South Carolina in 1785, declares that "The hatchet shall be forever buried, and the peace given by the United States . . . on the one part, and all the Cherokees on the other, shall be universal." Just two generations later, the US government expelled the Cherokees from their ancient homeland in the Trail of Tears, the act of ethnic cleansing that President Andrew Jackson's forked tongue had tried to obscure. Only a few Cherokees tried to "dig up the hatchet," a lesser-known phrase that suggests a resumption of war.

Sometimes the obvious source of an idiom is not the real one. That's the case with "making a killing," a phrase that sounds as if the only question about its origin would be which bloodthirsty war spawned it. Not so. It means a large profit in a business venture, and it began as a gambling expression. A Texas magazine first printed the phrase in 1888, referring to a gentleman who had won a substantial amount of money in a Louisiana lottery, or, as the article put it, "the man who was fortunate enough to 'make a killing.'"

War is, however, the genuine source of many expressions that are widely used in the business world, from "keeping your head down" to "joining forces." "It's no accident that many business strategies and management techniques were first developed in the military," the text on a Business English website states. "Companies fight each other for market share. We strategize about how to win the battle. You try to attack my market position, and I defend it. Business is full of such war idioms. Though it's not the only way we think about business, it is certainly the main way we talk about it." In that light, business idioms and sports idioms share a close affinity. The urge to defeat an opponent and emerge victorious means that in both realms, the language of war plays a prominent role.

"Loose lips sink ships," Americans said during the Second World War, and a few of them have gone on saying it ever since. The expression was invented by some clever wordsmith in the US War Advertising Council. It's a fancier way of saying "Keep silent" or, as the British put it, "Keep mum." During the same conflict, the British propaganda arm was responsible for posters with a witty slogan that is also appallingly sexist—"Be like Dad: keep Mum."

Compared to "Loose lips sink ships," other naval-gazing phrases are older and less obvious. "Tell it to the marines," for example, is like "about-face" in that it goes back to the Napoleonic Wars, the marines in question being not American but British. I always thought the idiom implied a belief that the marines would know better than to credit a barefaced lie; in fact, it means the reverse. A marine was a soldier stationed on a naval vessel, and as an English novelist named John Davis wrote in 1804, in the first recorded use of the phrase, "He may tell that to the marines, but the sailors will not believe him." Marines were seen as gullible neophytes, while sailors were hardened skeptics. If you look a speaker in the eye and say, "Tell it to the marines," you're showing that you don't believe the person.

The expression "nail your colors to the mast" comes from the same period. It now suggests a willingness to declare your beliefs openly, without subterfuge, although its original meaning suggested a defiant desire to fight on against the odds. Nautical colors, or flags, would be lowered in naval battles when a captain surrendered. But if the colors (or their remnants) were raised onto a mast (or the remains of a mast), the battle would continue. When a warship returned to port triumphant, its colors would be flying high for all on land to see. It was a public symbol of success, and the source of the familiar expression "pass with flying colors."

One of the potential dangers faced by sailors on board a wooden fighting ship involved a cannon breaking free of its restraining ropes, its heavy metal rolling wildly across the deck. This was the original "loose cannon." Today, we apply the expression to anyone whose statements or actions are deeply unpredictable. On board ship, cannons needed to be tied down, and so did scuttlebutts. A scuttlebutt was a cask of fresh water kept on deck, somewhere that sailors would gather for a drink. Standing around the scuttlebutt, they exchanged rumors and gossip. As time passed, "scuttlebutt" became a slang term not for the water, nor for the cask, but for the gossip and rumors.

No war has given the English language so many lasting idioms as the terrible four-year struggle that convulsed Europe and other parts of the globe between 1914 and 1918. At the time it was simply called the Great War. Over seventeen million people died during the fighting, and many more were wounded. The outbreak of another, even more catastrophic war in 1939 meant that the previous conflict has become known as the First World War. To it, we owe terms like "trench coat" (a padded waterproof coat that soldiers wore in the trenches) as well as new meanings for old expressions like "booby trap" (a harmless prank or practical joke back in the nineteenth century).

It's hard to imagine the long-drawn-out conflict on the Western Front without thinking of the space between the opposing trenches: no-man's-land. This was a very old phrase referring to a desolate area of waste ground, but it took on a specific military meaning during the First World War. In its horrific battles, soldiers were regularly ordered to leave the relative safety of their trenches and charge across no-man's-land to grab some ridge or thicket from the enemy. Today the expression can refer to any sort of nowhere zone, geographical or psychological. In March 2017, for example, one of the major newspapers in Texas published a feature article about the lives of people along the US-Mexico border; the article carried the headline "Living in No Man's Land."

As the soldiers clambered out of the trenches, they went "over the top." The phrase was born on the battlefields of the First World War and soon came to mean any unreasonable or excessive behavior. The operation would always commence at "zero hour." That expression, too, has expanded far beyond its military beginnings. In contemporary Britain, a "zero hour contract" means a casual arrangement in the labor market where an employee works without security, benefits, fixed hours or a minimum wage.

Spoonfuls of sugar

War entails serious insanity. Among the minor symptoms is the renaming of familiar places and things to avoid any positive thoughts of the enemy. In the United States, near the end of the First World War, sauerkraut became known as "liberty cabbage." German shepherds were renamed "Alsatians" by the British in the same period, Alsace being a contested region on the border of France and Germany. And in Canada, the city of Berlin changed its name to Kitchener in honor of Britain's recently deceased secretary of state for war. All these are forerunners of the absurd attempt in the United States to transform french fries into "freedom fries" when France refused to join the disastrous invasion of Iraq in 2003.

It was supposed to be "the war to end war," or "the war to end all wars." But that's not how the 1914–1918 conflict played out. As the initial promises—from both sides—of a quick victory faded into the reluctant acceptance of a prolonged stalemate, new expressions to express the unpleasant reality began to come to the fore. "In a flap"—worried, upset, anxious—dates from those years. Although the phrase has faded over the past few decades, it gave rise to the adjective "unflappable," still used to describe a calm person who reacts well in a crisis. The expression "nose dive" narrowly predates the First World War, but the conflict made the phrase famous. At first it referred only to an airplane's steep descent. Now you might hear it said about everything from the stock market or the value of the dollar to a party's standing in the latest opinion polls.

And what of the soldiers themselves? What they saw, heard and felt during the war gave many of them shell shock. An earlier expression for the same condition was "battle fatigue," but "shell shock" is more vivid and graphic. In the twenty-first century, with our mania for exactness and our fondness for acronyms, we're more likely to talk about PTSD (post-traumatic stress disorder). The notion of shell shock has been trivialized, normalized, tamed, so that nowadays it's as likely to refer to a sports team after a humiliating loss as it is to the survivors of a Syrian massacre.

But this is what language does. It subverts; it undercuts; it moves on. It took the phrase "basket case"—a soldier in the First World War who had somehow kept his life while losing most or all of his limbs, and therefore had to be carried around—and turned it into an idiom for anyone in a hopeless position. Language shows no respect. It can soften the hardest truths. And with warfare, that's what it consistently does.

Some of the most familiar idioms that we associate with the Second World War (1939–1945) are, in point of fact, older than the conflict itself. They were already hanging around the fringes of the English language, as though waiting for a chance at fame. Hitler's war gave them just what they needed.

Take the expression "concentration camp." It will always be linked to the Holocaust inflicted on European Jews and other minorities. But decades earlier, the phrase had referred to camps that the British set up in South Africa to imprison Afrikaner civilians during the Second Boer War. And before that, during the Cuban war of independence against Spain, it referred to the terror inflicted by the Spanish military on the inhabitants of Cuba, including the destruction of their crops and the forced concentration of people in a few small areas. As many as one in ten Cubans died as a result. "American citizens," proclaimed an Indiana newspaper in 1897, "must not be starved or otherwise executed in Spanish concentration camps in Cuba." This appears to be the first known use of the term.

"Storm troopers" were members of the Nazi militia, right? True, but not to begin with. The expression goes back to 1918, the final year of the First World War, at which time it described elite German soldiers trained to carry out sudden attacks. The original storm troops were fighting for Kaiser Wilhelm, not

Hitler. The word renewed its lease on life with the *Star Wars* movies, where it refers to soldiers of the Galactic Empire. As a story on a 2017 fansite breathlessly declared, "Sometimes a little villainy is what you need to complete an outfit, and these upcoming Stormtrooper boots make it easy for *Star Wars* fans."

And what of D-day? We think of it as June 6, 1944, the day of the Allied landings in northern France that began the liberation of much of Europe from Nazi rule. "D-day" was a code name for the Allied invasion. But like "storm troopers," the term had first been used in 1918. That year, a field order of the American Expeditionary Forces stated, "The First Army will attack at H-Hour on D-Day with the object of forcing the evacuation of St. Mihiel salient." (H-Hour referred to a particular hour on the designated day.) Almost a century later, a Scottish newspaper ran an article with the headline "D-Day for Women Battling to Get Breast Cancer Drug." Any fateful day—any fateful deadline—can now be portrayed as D-day. The inherent drama of war makes war-related idioms a tempting resource for reporters and editors.

Household Names

Wherever the American military went in the Second World War, there were liable to be drawings of a big-nosed, bald man accompanied by the scribbled phrase "Kilroy was here." No piece of graffiti has ever been so popular. Legend has it that in the final weeks of the war, at the Potsdam summit meeting where Joseph Stalin met Harry Truman and Winston Churchill, Stalin relieved himself in an exclusive toilet and emerged demanding to know who Kilroy was.

"Kilroy was here" is not so much an idiom as a *meme*—a word invented by the biologist Richard Dawkins to mean "a unit of cultural transmission, or a unit of *imitation* . . . Examples of memes are tunes, ideas, catchphrases, clothes fashions, ways of making pots or of building arches." Some people argue that the original Kilroy was a Massachusetts shipyard inspector named James J. Kilroy who marked his name on warships as they were being built, but others say that the phrase had been scrawled in Fort Knox in 1937. Whatever the truth, the American words merged with the cartoon face of a British equivalent, "Mr. Chad," to create the meme that so baffled Stalin.

One word that truly does have its origins in the Second World War is "flak." At first it meant one of the German army's powerful antiaircraft guns, the word being a radical British shortening of *Fliegerabwehrkanone*. As early as 1944, the American Dialect Society defined *flak-happy* as "the mental confusion of an airman exposed to severe *flak*." Soon the word moved beyond its military beginnings and began to mean fierce criticism in politics, business, sports or any other sphere of life. The renowned director Martin Scorsese once told an interviewer how glad he was that his controversial film *The Last Temptation of Christ* "was financed in Hollywood, that it's an American movie, that an American studio was willing to take the flak." "Taking the flak" has become a normal hazard of decision-making.

Long before the Second World War, "sights" referred to a device on a firearm that helped a gunman take aim. During and after the war, the word acquired a metaphorical overlay. To "raise your sights" meant to expand your goals or your dreams; to "lower your sights" meant the reverse. A mere five years after the Second World War had ended, *The Economist* declared that "The United States must now raise its sights, in terms of both manpower and production." Likewise, to "set your sights" on something no longer means, as it originally did, to be prepared to fire a gun at it. All these expressions have entered "civvy street": moved from military status, that is, into the civilian realm.

"Gung ho"—zealous, passionate or wildly enthusiastic—has one of the strangest origins of any expression. The phrase entered English via the US Marines and gained instant popularity during the Second World War thanks to a violent Hollywood movie entitled *Gung Ho!* The movie depicted a small group of Americans outwitting and killing Japanese troops on a remote Pacific island. Before it became a movie title, "gung ho" was the battle cry and motto of the Marine Raiders, as US commandos were then called; their leader, Lieutenant Colonel Evans Carlson, had introduced it to the soldiers in his charge. In the late 1930s, Carlson had served in China, where he was impressed by the Communist resistance to the Japanese invaders. He believed "gung ho" meant "work together" or "work in harmony." But he was wrong. The term is a shortened version of Gōngyè Hézuò: the English name for Chinese Industrial Cooperative Society, a movement that promoted economic development in the 1930s and 1940s.

The main founder of that organization, Carlson's friend Rewi Alley, was a New Zealander who spent most of his adult life in China. Alley was a gay man and a gung ho Communist. Hollywood had no idea what its Marines were yelling.

It Is Written

When you hear the expression "blood, sweat and tears," do you think of a rock band? (They've been going strong for half a century.) The band's name is also an idiom that means, in essence, an awful lot of hard work. Nothing will come easy, the phrase suggests. Winston Churchill is often cited as the source of the expression. In 1940, soon after becoming Britain's prime minister, he gave a famous speech in which he warned the nation of the sacrifices that would be required to defeat Nazi Germany.

But the phrase had been coined a long time earlier. In 1649, the poet William Drummond wrote a history of Scotland's kings in which he criticized their willingness "to draw such extraordinary subsidies from the blood, sweat, and tears of their people." Both Drummond and Churchill were relying on a much earlier image: Jesus, on the night before his death, went to pray on the Mount of Olives near Jerusalem. There, it's said, "Being in an agony he prayed more earnestly: and his sweat was as it were great drops of blood falling down to the ground."

On occasion, an idiom begins life as the title of a book. John le Carré popularized, though he may not have invented, the metaphorical use of "come in from the cold" (solitude, exile, exclusion) in his classic 1963 novel *The Spy Who Came in from the Cold*. The novel mostly takes place in Berlin during the Cold War, making the title a bitter pun. Joni Mitchell's song "Come In from the Cold" is likewise about the betrayal of youthful hope, the desire to make a difference in the world, and the disillusion brought by experience. The cold in the song is not the winter of her prairie girlhood.

But the outstanding example of a novel that became a byword in the English language is *Catch-22*. The author, Joseph Heller, had spent two years in the Second World War stationed in the Mediterranean, where he served as a crew member on bombing missions for the US Army Air Corps. His sardonic antiwar novel, first published in 1961, relied on a phrase that gave a new twist to old expressions like "Heads I win, tails you lose" and "Damned if you do, damned if you don't." A catch-22, as described in the novel, is a paradox that faced aircrews: bombing missions were so dangerous that if an airman asked to be exempt on the grounds of insanity, he proved he was sane. Only the mad would request to fly. Either way, there was no escape. Over time, the phrase "catch-22" has stretched its meaning so that now it often refers to any difficult or unwelcome choice.

You'd think that something as destructive as bombs would have a clear and obvious metaphorical meaning. Alas, no. In the US entertainment industry, the last thing you want is for a movie or TV show to bomb—a film that fails to come even close to breaking even is known as a "box office bomb." But in Britain, "go down a bomb" (or like a bomb) means "to be very successful or popular." The expression "bomb squad" also has contradictory meanings. It usually denotes a unit of the army or police force responsible for neutralizing explosives—but it can also refer to a terrorist group that plants the explosives.

It's time to "bite the bullet"—a British phrase dating from the eighteenth century—and look at idioms about war itself. War can be a stereotype, an archetype, a prototype. It has been part of history since the beginning and, alas, it shows no sign of disappearing anytime soon. No wonder it's intrinsic to a multitude of phrases and idioms.

"On the warpath" goes back to the trails that indigenous North Americans would follow on their way to battle. These days, it can mean any kind of determined or ugly campaign: "Kardashian Sisters on the Warpath After Caitlyn Trashes Their Dad" was a recent tabloid headline. Tabloids delight in "wars of words," conflicts fought not with guns but with pens (or, in our day, with tablets, iPhones and laptops). A "war of nerves" might be any campaign in which the psychology of the combatants is of supreme importance. And if the campaign is at a stage of advanced preparation, the participants are said to be on a war footing.

An old British phrase, "in the wars," shows some recognition of the suffering that wars provoke. As a graphic synonym for hurt or injured, it's still current in much of the English-speaking world, although not in North America. In March 2017, an Irish newspaper reported on the latest match of the national soccer team by saying "Whelan was in the wars and required a head bandage after Aaron Ramsey caught him with a high boot." That's one kind of turf war. More generally, "turf war" refers to a struggle over territory being fought by rival gangs, parties or businesses. To win a turf war, or an election, a group may need to bolster its resources—or, you might say, build up its war chest.

Among the most poignant of all military expressions is "warhorse." Four hundred years ago, if you had called an animal a warhorse, you would have been paying it a compliment: it meant a powerful horse ridden in battle by a knight or high-ranking officer. Gradually the word came to mean a veteran actor, a reliable old politician, or any older person. "She's an old warhorse, is your mother": that line was printed in 1898 in a newspaper in Portland, Oregon. A century later, the magazine *Travel & Leisure* could publish a restaurant review describing shrimp cocktail and onion soup as "traditional warhorses." The English book and play *War Horse*, adapted into a 2011 movie by Steven Spielberg, restored an older meaning to the phrase: it was about a real horse in a real army in a real conflict, the First World War.

A Portuguese man-of-war, by contrast, is an assemblage of brightly colored invertebrates with venomous tentacles, distantly related to a jellyfish. (It's also known as a "floating terror.") Supposedly the creature bears a remote resemblance to the Lisbon version of an eighteenth-century sailing vessel known as a man-of-war. In the Japanese language, the animal's name translates literally as "skipjack tuna's priestly hat." That may sound ridiculous. But is it any more ridiculous than naming a tropical invertebrate after a European warship?

Spoonfuls of sugar

Few words are acronyms: they have not been tossed together from the initial letters of other words. Don't believe anyone who tells you that the most familiar four-letter word in the English language is short for "Fornication Under Consent of the King"—in fact, the word goes back many hundreds of years and is related to similar terms in German, Dutch, Norwegian and Swedish.

A handful of English words, however, really are acronyms. "Snafu" is one of them. It means chaotic or confused, often with a wry implication that chaos is the natural order of things. Soldiers invented the term during the Second World War, using the first letters of words in the phrase "Situation normal, all f***ed up." (Sometimes it's expressed in G-rated form as "Situation normal, all fouled up" but trust me on this, the G-rated version is not the original.) "AWOL"—usually written in capital letters, though sometimes now simply "Awol"—also has its origin in the US military. It's an older term, one dating from the late nineteenth century. Then, as now, for a soldier to be "absent without official leave" was cause for punishment.

And what about military language now? Considering the enormous numbers of people who serve in the armed forces, especially in the United States, it's a little surprising that more of today's military expressions haven't pushed their way into everyday speech. Still, a few idioms have crossed over, and more will surely do so.

"Sandbox" or "sandpit" is US military jargon for Iraq or, occasionally, other countries in the Middle East. The flourlike powder that covers much of the land in Iraq and Afghanistan—especially around US military bases, once the giant construction vehicles have had their way—has the evocative name "moon dust." "Forward operating bases" are commonly abbreviated to FOBs. Combine that term with the heroes of J. R. R. Tolkien's fantasy novels, and you have the new word "fobbit," military slang for soldiers who do not venture out on patrol beyond the safety of the base.

Soldiers in the British Army now use the phrase "This is bone" to mean anything they consider pointless. As a former captain in the Coldstream Guards wrote in 2015, "I always thought ironing combats was one of the most bone things I had to do." (Combats, in that sentence, means "combat fatigues," a type of uniform.) Among US forces, on the other hand, "bone" is slang for the supersonic B-1 bomber. "Weekend warrior" has a civilian meaning (somebody who engages in sporting activities only on Saturdays and Sundays), but it carries a military sense, too: a reservist in the US armed forces. And "secret squirrel," originally the name of a TV cartoon show, can refer to any classified information or top-secret job. In 2014, when President Obama opened secret negotiations with the government of Cuba, the talks were known as Project Ardilla, the Spanish word for squirrel.

Some of these military phrases are cute. But none of them comes to grips with the overwhelming force of modern weapons or the dangers posed by terrorism and nuclear war. It's as if we find these topics either impossible to imagine or too painful to think about. Normally so full of invention, language recoils from this kind of thinking and feeling. A term that was, ironically enough, invented to describe the impact of the atomic bombs dropped on Japan in 1945—"ground zero"—went on to be an expression associated with the terrorist attacks on New York in 2001. For the next few years, "ground zero" was seldom uttered except with reference to the former World Trade Center. Yet by 2017, *Outdoor Life* magazine could give a feature article the headline "Florida's Indian River Was Ground Zero of America's Bloody Conservation History." "Ground zero" can now mean almost any sort of base or birthplace.

In April 2017, the US Air Force dropped the largest non-nuclear bomb in its arsenal on a remote area in eastern Afghanistan. The weapon is officially known as a GBU-43/B Massive Ordnance Air Blast. But who could remember a name like that? Military terms are notoriously, and deliberately, technical: the more they include initials, numbers and stray punctuation, the less likely people are to understand what's meant. As far as I know, the US military does not have a widely understood name for the version of its CBU-55A/B cluster bomb that has three BLU-73A/B submunitions in a SUU-49A/B dispenser. Technical vocabulary adds precision. It also detaches a weapon from its purpose: death.

The bomb that was dropped from the Afghan sky in April 2017 weighed nearly eleven tons. It exploded before reaching the ground, creating a massive fireball and a huge pressure wave. Never before had this weapon been used against an enemy.

It is, unusually, a weapon with a nickname. Take the initials of Massive Ordnance Air Blast, mix in a hefty dose of shock and awe, and you end up with the memorable phrase "Mother of All Bombs." The US military first tested it in 2003, after which the Russian military presumably felt inadequate: four years later they tested an even larger weapon that has the nickname "Father of All Bombs."

"Not to be outdone," wrote former Congressman Dennis Kucinich, "the U.S. has taken steps to have a new 'mother' brought forward, this one weighing 30,000 pounds.

"How unbelievable it is to live in a time where the life-creating symbols of mother and father became the agencies of the destruction of life. Our metaphors are signposts to the end of the world."

Can a Leopard Change Its Spots?

We've seen that idioms help maintain the rich and diverse flavors of English. They keep language from being leached out over time; without idioms, language would be thin and watery. Idioms can make us laugh. They can make us think, too.

But they also serve another function, one I haven't mentioned yet. To explain, I need to introduce an idiom that is also a concept: "plastic words."

Do your eyes glaze over when you read an official document issued by a government, a university or a corporation? Mine do. Here's one stupor-inducing example, which I found on the website of the World Trade Organization: "The WTO provides a forum for negotiating agreements aimed at reducing obstacles to international trade . . . thus contributing to economic growth and development. The WTO also provides a legal and institutional framework for the implementation and monitoring of these agreements, as well as for settling disputes arising from their interpretation and application." I'm sorry: that was boring to read, although it's less convoluted than the ponderous rhetoric that emerges from many institutions.

The WTO statement is composed almost entirely of what Uwe Poerksen calls "plastic words." Poerksen, a German linguist and literary scholar, coined the phrase in a 1988 book that has become ever more resonant as the years pass. His book—entitled, in translation, *Plastic Words: The Tyranny of a Modular Language*—is a devastating critique of the kind of bloodless, abstract language often favored by big institutions. The term "modular" in the subtitle is apt because so many of the elements of plastic language are interchangeable: a noun can morph into a verb or an adjective as easily as a middle manager changes positions in a big company.

Plastic words like *development* and *implementation* can mean everything or nothing. They're the opposite of idiomatic speech. In annual reports, corporate press releases, grant applications and countless other white-collar documents, plastic words exude an air of professional competence. They are useful at disguising the truth—at hiding some goal or action behind a mask of bland efficiency. For instance, Correctional Service Canada—the country's federal prison system—no longer uses the expression "solitary confinement"; instead, it refers to "administrative segregation." (Who knows what takes place in the system's "annual regional administrative segregation compliance reviews"?) As Poerksen writes, "Abstract language serves to cover up reality. It prevents the imagination from reflecting on what actually happens to people. It ignores what they experience and what they feel, their life histories." He argues that generic terms like "research" and "communication," "progress" and "community" exert a subtle tyranny over the ways we see and feel our world.

But plastic words like these are absent from idioms. Idioms crystallize the emotions that people have felt over time—emotions that are raw and messy, not modular. Instead of generalizing about "communication," idioms warn us that bad news travels fast, suggest that no news is good news (or good news is no news), and propose that truth is stranger than fiction. Rather than analyzing "municipalities," idioms distinguish between cardboard city and easy street, and tell us that it takes a village to raise a child.

Nobody in the world, I suspect, has a deeply felt life story with "administrative" or "implementation" in it. By contrast, feelings and perceptions are powerfully expressed in the kind of physical, down-to-earth language that idioms grant us. They make connections. They forge relationships. "An original and imaginative metaphor," writes the American poet Rebecca McClanahan, "brings something fresh into the world. In the interaction between two things being compared, a new image or idea is formed."

Still, we have to be careful not to jump from the frying pan into the fire—from plastic words into clichés, that is.

A cliché is a figure of speech that discourages original thinking. It stops ideas in their tracks—or it guides ideas along a single well-worn track. The literal meaning is relevant: in the early nineteenth century, a cliché was a method of printing an engraving, using a solid plate of metal. That plate had the name "stereotype." Being a duplicate from the outset, a stereotype would perpetuate an original form without allowing any change. Both these terms were originally French, a fact that English speakers have done their best to ignore. (Ernest Bevin, a British cabinet minister, once rejected a draft speech by saying "This will not do . . . It just goes on from clitch to clitch.") Printers in the past used clichés and stereotypes to provide for the mass reproduction of images. In our own time, politicians, governments and corporations often find the mass reproduction of stock phrases to be a very useful tactic.

Songwriters are fond of clichés, too.

Nineteen seventy was a good year for popular music. From "Bridge Over Troubled Water" to "Lola," from "Big Yellow Taxi" to "My Sweet Lord," memorable songs poured out across the airwaves of the English-speaking world. A number of them spoke directly or indirectly about pressing topics of the day—gender issues, spiritual quests, pollution, the Vietnam War. (Many of them were about sex, too.) But despite their quality and their impact, only a few of the best songs of 1970 approached the sales figures racked up by a young country singer named Lynn Anderson. Her version of "Rose Garden" was a country-pop crossover hit with a catchy tune and a set of lyrics made up almost entirely of clichés.

Think I'm exaggerating? Then consider the following phrases, all of which the song invokes:

Sharing the good times. Promising the moon. Sweet talk. Still waters that run deep. Smiling for a while. Looking before you leap. Dreams of silver platters and diamond rings combine with the recurrent image of a rose garden to create a familiar backdrop for the secondhand emotions on which, then and now, Top 40 radio thrives.

Few pop songs are immune to clichés. But while many songs include a few clichés, "Rose Garden" contains little else. Even on a single hearing, its lyrics are as routine and reassuring as a double cheeseburger with french fries on the side. They offer no challenges, raise no questions, incite no debates. The song serves up the verbal equivalent of high-carb comfort food in words that are neither abstract nor original. "Rose Garden" was massively popular. Familiarity doesn't always breed contempt—it can also breed large record sales.

Apart from their role in paying songwriters' mortgages, clichés have their uses. In his book *Words, Words, Words*, the linguist David Crystal mounts a shrewd defense of them: "They can fill an awkward gap in a conversation. They can be a lexical lifejacket when we are stuck for something to say . . . Think of the required politeness of regular commuters on a train. Think of the forced interactions at cocktail parties. Or the desperate platitudes which follow a funeral. These are the kinds of occasion which give clichés their right to be." These are solid practical justifications. But I think the power of clichés goes deeper.

At a time when many of us feel the world is spinning out of control, clichés offer a little much-needed consolation. If Earth could seem a nerve-racking planet in 1970, how much scarier it is today. Clichés and platitudes deliver a quick hit of Valium to the wounded soul. What goes around, comes around. The rest is history. It is what it is.

• • •

"Make it new," urged the poet Ezra Pound early in the twentieth century. He wanted writers to abandon vague, overfamiliar modes of expression and to explore fresh territories of speech. Pound's advice had a lasting influence—on the language used by poets, I mean, though not by many songwriters. Soon the quest for the new became a dominant impulse in modernist literature as it already was in painting, sculpture and classical music. "The sentence should be arbitrary," Gertrude Stein declared in *How to Write*. "A paragraph such as silly." But readers were skeptical from the outset.

Most of us don't seek out a new form of language, and if we happen to come across arbitrary sentences or silly paragraphs, we're less than thrilled about it. The old idioms work just fine. We know what they mean. Even if I store food in cartons in the fridge, I don't "keep all my eggs in one basket." Even if you never cook for yourself, you sometimes "put it on the backburner."

Does this mean that old idioms are inevitably clichéd?

Not in the least. What counts, as far as I'm concerned, is not the age of an idiom but the context that surrounds it and the way it's expressed. Compelling idioms have the power to keep language real. Any smart adaptation of a familiar expression can deliver a small jolt of surprise to readers or listeners. Warning against consumers' debt addiction in the *Guardian* in September 2017, Zoe Williams wrote: "We don't need any ailing canaries to tell us there's a gas leak: we need to start asking how to escape this mine." By taking the old image of a coal-mine canary into an article about the crushing weight of debt, Williams made her argument come alive.

Clichés do the reverse. They capture a morsel of thought, cover it in batter, and fry it into mush. It can be hard to figure out if an original perception lies buried under the greasy words. Sometimes this is inadvertent. But often it's deliberate—I'm sure Joe South, who wrote the lyrics to "Rose Garden," knew exactly what he was doing. "In songwriting," observes the singer/songwriter Blair Packham, "given the brevity of the medium—three minutes or so—you have to establish the setting or the premise of the song quickly. Sometimes, a well-placed cliché can help. And the very medium of pop music—of its time, meant to be of the moment—means, logically, that there is always a new audience coming along, unaware of clichéd words and phrases, willing to accept them at face value."

Donkey's Hind Leg

In his inaugural address in 1829, US president Andrew Jackson talked about "the sensibility belonging to a gallant people." The phrase "a gallant people" was a common tidbit of political rhetoric in the nineteenth century. A group of Washington citizens used it in a farewell address to Thomas Jefferson in 1809; a proslavery speaker in the US Senate described his fellow Southerners as "a gallant people"; Canadian prime minister Sir John A. Macdonald deployed the phrase in 1891, during his last major speech. By then, "a gallant people" had become a cliché, just like "the silent majority" during the Nixon presidency and "America First" in the Trump era.

"A gallant people" faded from sight during the twentieth century as the word *gallant* went out of fashion. If a man was gallant, did this mean he was daring, or brave, or fashionable, or well-mannered, or attentive to women, or some combination of all those qualities? Uncertainty about the meaning of *gallant* meant that "a gallant people" ceased to be a cliché. If a politician revived the expression now, it would be surprising. It might even sound original.

For the powerful, the repetition of stock phrases can be a valuable tactic. These phrases serve to fortify rhetorical armor, deflecting all attack. The armor often brings clichés and plastic words together in a metallic professional embrace. Consider this, from an article on the website of the British government: "The Prime Minister emphasised her desire to listen to the views of businesses, to channel their experience and to share with them the government's vision for a successful Brexit and a country in which growth and opportunity is shared by everyone across the whole of the UK." Or this, from a speech by the CEO of Exxon Mobil: "Our job is to compete and succeed in any market, regardless of conditions or price. To do this, we must produce and deliver the highest-value products at the lowest possible cost through the most attractive channels in all operating environments."

To quote neither the Bible nor William Shakespeare: yada yada yada.

"The great enemy of clear language is insincerity," George Orwell wrote in 1946. "When there is a gap between one's real and one's declared aims, one turns . . . to long words and exhausted idioms, like a cuttlefish squirting out ink." In his brilliant essay "Politics and the English Language," Orwell gave some lively examples of what a "tired hack on the platform" was, in his time, likely to say: "bestial atrocities, iron heel, bloodstained tyranny, free peoples of the world, stand shoulder to shoulder." A few of those expressions have become less prevalent over time, but others remain current. Presidents and prime ministers still boast about standing shoulder to shoulder, even while they knife each other in the back.

On July 1, 2017, the 150th anniversary of Canada's birth as a nation, Prime Minister Justin Trudeau delivered an outdoor address before thousands of people on Parliament Hill in Ottawa. The text of his speech was riddled with plastic words and clichés: "The story of Canada is really the story of ordinary people doing extraordinary things . . . Canadians know that better is always possible . . . Our job now is to advance equal opportunity to ensure that each and every Canadian has a real and fair chance at success." These are worthy sentiments. They're also numbingly familiar—Trudeau's language could have been lifted from a thousand other speeches, and probably was. As Orwell put it, "If you use ready-made phrases, you not only don't have to hunt about for words; you also don't have to bother with the rhythms of your sentences, since these phrases are generally so arranged as to be more or less euphonious." Listeners can be lulled into smiling submission.

Or they can be roused to a condition of prefabricated outrage. Clichés help in that process, too. A few weeks after Trudeau's address, the governor of Texas, Greg Abbott, spoke at a sheriffs' convention in a city named Grapevine. "Respect for our law enforcement officers must be restored in our nation," he said. "The badge every sheriff and every officer wear over his or her heart is a reminder of a sacred trust, commitment and contract with each of us. For law enforcement to stand in front of us and all that threatens, we must stand behind them. It is time for us to unite as Texans and as Americans and to say no more—no more will we tolerate disrespect for those who serve, and no more will we allow the evil merchants of hate tear us apart." Abbott's grammar was shaky but the trajectory of his rhetoric was clear. His repeated use of "must," combined with clichés like "evil merchants of hate," allowed for no dissent. Standing at a podium in a business suit and tie, the governor bore a distinct resemblance to a cuttlefish squirting out ink.

An equally troubling type of political language is the "dog whistle"—an idiom born in the 1980s, although the practice it refers to is much older. The expression draws on the idea that dogs hear and respond to high-frequency noises beyond the reach of human ears. It means the use of coded messages to reach certain targeted groups, without the rest of the public being aware what's going on. Those messages may rely on idioms. In 2016, Kellie Leitch, a candidate to lead Canada's Conservative Party, surveyed potential supporters on whether immigrants should be screened for what she called "anti-Canadian values." One of her rivals for the leadership, Michael Chong, denounced the idea as "dog-whistle politics." The phrase "anti-Canadian values" told Conservative voters that Leitch would be the right leader to stop Muslim immigration, without the candidate needing to spell it out.

Dog-whistle expressions are an example of the unpleasant use idioms are sometimes put to. But in a repressive society, words, images and idioms can play a subversive role. China blocked all social media references to Winnie-the-Pooh in 2017—the honey-loving bear had become an online euphemism for the country's president, Xi Jinping, who is short and pudgy. When bloggers in China post an image of a river crab, they're almost certainly referring to censorship. Why? Because "harmonized" and "river crab" are both *hexie* in Chinese—the words differ only in tone. And after the previous president, Hu Jintao, spoke repeatedly about promoting a harmonized society, "river crab" turned into a symbolic substitute for "censored."

Sometimes the line between idiom and cliché gets blurred. Various expressions that I've cited earlier in this book have appeared on lists of clichés—"Cut off your nose to spite your face," "Wear your heart on your sleeve," "A few sandwiches short of a picnic," and more. But are these really clichés?

I don't think so. If all those expressions were clichés, we could come under fire for speaking in any kind of figurative terms. The distinction between an idiom and a cliché is partly subjective, but it depends too on the rate and type of usage. The three idioms mentioned above do not appear on smartphones, laptops, tablets, TV sets and newspapers with anything like the frequency of, let's say, "silver platter" or "still waters run deep." Yet they're not unknown to us. For an idiom to be broadly understood, it needs to be occasionally heard or read. All three of those expressions would bemuse a newcomer to English. They make sense to us only because we've met them before.

We don't want to run into them too often, though—repetition of any phrase can turn it into a cliché. If we're always using the same line, perhaps we're not as free as we like to think. Clichés are, by definition, recurrent: they encourage us to think and speak along predictable tracks. When the tracks turn into wheel ruts, it's a challenge to steer out of them. We may find ourselves stuck in a verbal furrow, saying: "At the end of the day, let's face the facts: I'm giving it 110 percent." But when people hear an expression like "drain the swamp" day after day, how long does it take before they begin to accept what the speaker means by those words? If idioms help us think outside the box, clichés box us in.

"The straw that breaks the camel's back" is an expression that has worn out most of its welcome by overuse. It's the winning variant, so to speak, from among a long list of similar idioms, the oldest of them being "the feather that breaks the horse's back." Over the centuries, other versions included "the straw that breaks the donkey's back," "the peppercorn that breaks the camel's back," and "the melon that breaks the monkey's back" (this one made the most sense, and therefore had little chance of success). In August 2017, a story on the CBC News website tried to twist the idiom into something fancier than a cliché by saying that the new government of British Columbia had decided to place "more regulatory and legal straws on the camel that is the Trans Mountain pipeline." Sorry, but no matter how you look at it, a pipeline is not a camel.

Still, it's possible to subvert a cliché if listeners are reminded of its literal meaning as well as its figurative sense. One routine expression for trouble is "in hot water." When CNN asked the environmentalist Bill McKibben in 2017 about two new reports on the severity of climate change, he replied: "These studies are part of the emerging scientific understanding that we're in even hotter water than we'd thought." Perhaps McKibben was deploying a figure of speech in a clever way, drawing attention to the gravity of the issue by giving physical meaning to an old idiom. Or perhaps he was undermining his message by resorting to a cliché.

Household Names

Ancient legends say that Achilles, the great hero of Homer's *Iliad*, believed himself to be invulnerable. His mother, an immortal nymph, dipped him in the sacred river Styx when he was a baby so that all the parts of his body touched by water would be immune to decay or attack. But the nymph was holding her infant son by one of his heels—the same spot where, many years later during the Trojan War, a poisoned arrow broke his flesh. The wound was fatal. This story gave rise to the expression "Achilles' heel"—a weak point that can prove ruinous. The phrase has now become so common, and is used in so many circumstances, that it seems to have obtained cliché status.

The idiom gave its name, in turn, to a related body part. The tendons that pass through the feet and lower legs are the thickest in the body, and if one of them is ruptured, the damage can be hard to repair. Basketball star Isiah Thomas was one of many athletes forced to retire after injuring an Achilles tendon.

The idea of the cliché has now become pervasive far beyond the printing business and the word trade. It proved so valuable there that it elbowed its way into other realms, too. Russian villains and far-fetched car chases are said to be clichés in Hollywood movies. Appearances of the Russian villain may be accompanied in the soundtrack by a dark, brooding melody played in a minor key: a musical cliché. Scenes of cute girls and boys dispensing advice to their hapless parents have become a cliché in TV advertising. These examples are, if you like, nonverbal idioms, all of them predictable in their tone and implications, all of them beset by overuse.

In some contexts, alas, the use of clichés is the rule, not the exception. If you've ever listened to an interview with a professional hockey player, you'll know what I mean. The Stanley Cup–winning goal in 2014 was scored in double overtime by a Los Angeles Kings' defenseman named Alec Martinez, and following the game, Martinez was asked how the Kings had reacted after falling behind their opponents late in the second period. "We just did it by committee," he said. "We've got great leadership in our locker-room and, you know, we've been in that situation before. Obviously, it's not the situation you want going into the locker-room after the second, but we came out and battled back."

A few minutes after the most thrilling moment of his career, if not his life, Martinez was still talking in dull stock phrases: "by committee . . . leadership in our locker-room . . . been in that situation . . . obviously . . . came out and battled back." Sad to say, the avoidance of personal language has become part of the culture of most professional sports. Yogi Berra's unique style of speaking was memorable not just because he made some hilarious mistakes but because he spoke candidly and personally. "We were overwhelming underdogs": Berra had a rare gift for turning clichés back into idioms.

Clichés are prominent in the stories that athletes repeat to outsiders. Unlike plastic words, they also appear in some of the stories we tell about ourselves. (Mission statements are full of them.) But to quote a proverb at least four centuries old, "one man's meat is another man's poison." What you deplore as a cliché, I may cherish as a soul-stirring idiom. In his 2008 election campaign, Barack Obama's defining slogan was "Yes, we can!" A cliché, some voters felt. Eight years later, Donald Trump's defining slogan was "Make America great again!" Was this an inspirational appeal or a dangerous cliché? The answer depends not only on the words themselves but on your own beliefs.

We saw at the start of this book how idioms are like repeated musical phrases. Good writers know how to use them in harmony with the other elements of a text. This analogy helps us to see why clichés are so annoying. A cliché is like an earworm—a tune that plays endlessly inside your head, refusing to leave you in peace. In a literal sense, clichés are monotonous: they have a single tone. They make the same point, over and over. They are like the Biblical leopard, unable to change his spots.

Combing the Giraffe

In 1982, when Maori activists in New Zealand set out to make sure their language would survive, they founded a *Kōhanga Reo* for preschool children who might otherwise never learn their ancestral tongue. The Maori expression literally translates into English as "language nest." The children spend much of their early life in the warm shelter of Maori values, words and caregivers. *Kōhanga Reo* have proved a tremendous success—there are now more than 460 of them across New Zealand, educating thousands of children.

They have inspired similar arrangements in Australia, the United States, Canada, and several European countries. These preschools generally derive their name from the same image, in their own language, that *Kōhanga Reo* gives in Maori. As a result, "language nest" has become an English expression and the concept has found words in other languages as far-flung as Hawaiian, Ojibway and Estonian.

Idioms, by contrast, lend themselves to a variety of tones. The verbal melodies they express may appear in unpredictable form. They are perpetually ready to shift shape. By uniting a physical image with an abstract thought, idioms can take their place in many different patterns. When you utter an expression that has startling idiomatic force, it can make your listeners or readers hear or see the world in a different way.

Think of what the renowned physicist Paul Davies wrote in a 2007 article about the origin of the cosmos. Can we do better, he asked readers of the *Guardian*, than "an unexplained God or an unexplained set of mathematical laws"? Indeed we can, Davies suggested, "but only by relinquishing the traditional idea of physical laws as fixed, perfect relationships. I propose instead that the laws are more like computer software: programs being run on the great cosmic computer. They emerge with the universe at the big bang and are inherent in it, not stamped on it from without like a maker's mark." Davies's words rely on idioms and figures of speech to make his ideas come to life.

In his earlier book *Mind of God*, Davies suggested that each age draws on its most impressive technology as a guiding metaphor to understand the cosmos and the divine. In ancient

Greece, where musical instruments were the height of technology, numbers and harmony were seen as essential to the workings of the universe—hence the idea of the "music of the spheres." In Isaac Newton's day, the mechanical achievements of time measurement provoked the notion of a clockwork universe, and in our digital age, physicists inspect the universe as if it were composed of data. Science is not exempt from idioms—metaphors, for Davies, pervade not just our speaking and writing but also our patterns of thinking.

I won't mince my words: idioms should be the talk of the town. They allow you to be creative in how you use them—it's not as if they're written in stone. When the word gets out, feel free to speak your mind. It's okay to change your tune from time to time. I won't make a song and dance about it, but there are many things worse than a slip of the lip. You may even get the last word.

Just remember: watch your tongue.

Acknowledgments

Between 2006 and 2017, I wrote a language column named "Watchwords" for the *Montreal Gazette*. I'm happy for the chance to thank Edie Austin, who hired me to write the column and who edited it meticulously. I'm equally grateful to all the readers who contacted me over the years, sharing their ideas, their questions and especially their pet peeves. The experience of writing "Watchwords" was enough to dispel any suspicion I had that so-called ordinary people don't care about language. They do: I have many hundreds of emails to prove it. Not a sentence in this book was lifted directly from "Watchwords," but the entire book is informed by what I learned over the decade of writing the column.

Watch Your Tongue was edited by Brendan May, and I'm profoundly grateful to him. His friendly yet firm editing had a great impact on the book. Brendan not only introduced me to idioms like "Netflix and chill," he gently shoved my prose into the second decade of the twenty-first century. I also want to thank Belle Wuthrich for her witty, discerning illustrations, and Laurie McGee and Martha Schwartz for their punctilious copyediting.

Jackie Kaiser, the president of Westwood Creative Artists, has worked hard and long on my behalf, giving me good advice even when I don't want to hear it. I'm honored and flattered that Jackie continues to represent me.

As always, I thank my family for their love, patience and support. My wife, Ann Beer, my son, Kayden, and my daughter, Megan, are a constant inspiration. They don't keep my shoulder to the wheel, but they do keep my feet on the ground.

Finally I want to thank my friends, not just for putting up with so much wordplay through the years but for encouraging it too. I hope this book proves to them that I'm more than just a flash in the pun.